Gordon Ramsay's
passion for seafood

with Roz Denny

photographs by Diana Miller
foreword by Daniel Boulud

conran
OCTOPUS

To my father Gordon Scott Ramsay for those
wonderful fishing trips on the River Tay.

First published in Great Britain in 1999 by
Conran Octopus Ltd
a part of Octopus Publishing Group
2–4 Heron Quays
London E14 4JP

www.conran-octopus.co.uk

Reprinted in 2000, 2002 (twice)

ISBN 1 84091 285 5

Managing Editor Kate Bell
Copy Editors Caroline Fraser Ker, Norma MacMillan
Editorial Assistant Alexandra Kent

Art Director Leslie Harrington
Home Economist Annie Nichols
Stylist Wei Tang
Typesetting Olivia Norton

Production Suzanne Sharpless

British Library Cataloguing-in-Publication Data
A catalogue record for this book is available from the
British Library

Colour origination by Sang Choy International,
Singapore. Printed and bound in Spain by
Artes Gráficas Toledo, S A U
D L TO 1458-2002

page 1: escabèche of sardines (page 94)
page 2: chilled melon and lobster soup
(page 89)
this page: smoked haddock, lentil and leek tart
(page 187)

Wine notes by Thierry Berson

contents

foreword

Seafood is one of the most difficult subjects for a chef to master, yet is one of the most rewarding once conquered. In a restaurant kitchen, the fish station is the most challenging and the most versatile. Fish is such a malleable ingredient to cook: it can be prepared to taste briny, sweet, fragrant, juicy, tangy, even meaty – a multitude of adjectives apply. It is up to the chef to find the appropriate attribute for the particular fish he or she is preparing to serve, and to perfect its taste through the precise method of cooking and the exact seasoning necessary.

Seafood is exciting to cook because of the choice one has in the final balance of taste, and is very challenging because there are so many possible combinations that one can create. Seafood can be so many things. One can enjoy the simple pleasure of a freshly shucked oyster with just a squirt of lemon or, on a completely different and much more complex level, a recipe such as Gordon's.Crab Ravioli with Sauce Vierge (page 138).

Gordon is a leading figure and an inspiration in the field of cooking in the United Kingdom. French cooking is still considered by many to be the mother of all cuisines, and Gordon has not only understood it completely but has used it as a springboard to create his own culinary identity. There is a wonderful depth and quality to his cooking which you will be able to discover for yourself either by visiting 68 Royal Hospital Road in London or by making one (or many) of the recipes in this book.

Gordon makes his achieved perfection seem homely and easy to attain, and has opened up his experience to the home cook by writing this comprehensive guide. In *Passion for Seafood* he has done a fabulous job of explaining the basics (from buying fish to cooking techniques). Once you are confident with these, he provides wonderful, innovative recipes to inspire you. I also think that a definite bonus for the home cook will be Gordon's idea of suggesting alternatives when the fish called for in the recipe is not available. Not only will this simplify matters, it will also be a nudge for you to take Gordon's recipes and make them your own. Improvization is an essential part of cooking and Gordon gives you the freedom to discover this within the confines of a structured recipe.

This book is a definite must for any (sea)food lover and passionate cook.

Bon appétit !

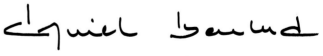

marinated tuna with balsamic-dressed mooli (page 112)

introduction

It is gradually dawning on me that seafood has been part of my life ever since I was a small boy. Not that I was brought up in a fishing community, or lived by the sea. But, looking back on my everyday sort of upbringing in Scotland, there were many instances where seafood made great impressions on my developing psyche – like the weekly Saturday trip to Glasgow's open air market as a small boy with my family. The reward for being good was to cram six of us on a bench in the packed winkle and cockle shop. Piles of steaming shells would be laid before us on newspaper, with bowls for the empties. Armed with pins, and working fast, we would pop the shelly discs off the tops of each winkle and carefully extract the corkscrew flesh. A quick seasoning of salt and malt vinegar and we'd down several at a time on a spoon.

My dad taught me to fish. We had a caravan on the shore of Loch Lomond and fishing became part of our summer lifestyle. When salmon went on the run to spawn, we'd be up at five in the morning to try our luck at catching a few. Threading wriggling blood worms as bait on to treble-hook traces, we would row out to the middle of the loch to set the lines using empty squeezy Jif Lemon bottles as floats. Then we rowed back to shore and waited. When those little yellow bottles started bobbing up and down, back we'd row and pick up our haul. One time we spent all morning chasing a large salmon, but what a beauty. Even now, a great treat is a day's fly fishing on the Tay. Occasionally, my brother and I also manage to sneak off together and enjoy night fishing at Minehead, burying ourselves in the shingle. Frozen squid make good bait to catch dogfish (rock salmon) and whiting.

During my time in Paris, training with Guy Savoy, there was fresh fish all around me. I would spend time wandering around the market at Rungis just gazing at the displays. Or get off two stops on the Metro before my flat and walk to the Boffinger seafood restaurant to watch the waiters on their own lunch breaks, wading through trays of fresh oysters with obvious enjoyment, and breathtaking speed – even though they spent all their working lives opening them for others.

Tropical fish or exotics – call them what you will – became part of my piscine education, working as the ship's cook on a luxury yacht in the Caribbean. There are no markets at sea and, with a hungry crew to feed three times a day, we had to go back to nature and catch our food. Diving also became an obsession, and I learnt about the habits of beautiful sea creatures beneath the waves.

The manta rays were the most magnificent as they wafted past with their billowing fins. Spiny lobsters are cunning crustaceans. I'm sure they've got a sneaking feeling we enjoy their sweet flesh. Night dives were the most fascinating. Did you know parrot fish blow out liquid bubbles to protect them as they sleep?

When we trapped cuttlefish in our nets, their flesh was so clear we could see veins moving inside. What we couldn't eat became bait to catch baby bonito tuna. Our favourite crew meal was huge clams grilled with lemon butter and served with fresh linguine (made on the boat – I still love making my own pasta each day).

All these experiences have left me with a lasting impression of the need to protect the wealth of the sea, from the powerful North Atlantic with its dwindling stocks of cod and white fish to the fragile, dreamlike beauty of the coral reefs. I may be a fisherman and cook these beautiful creatures each day but I have a very deep respect for their beauty and sustenance, and greatly appreciate the skills entrusted to me to do them justice. I certainly try hard to please.

notes for the cook

Standard metric spoon measures have been used for testing all the recipes: 1 teaspoon = 5 ml, 1 tablespoon = 15 ml. Spoons are measured level unless otherwise specified.

Medium eggs were used for testing unless otherwise specified.

Current recommendations are that children, pregnant women, the elderly and people on immuno-suppressant drugs should not eat raw or lightly cooked eggs because of the risk of contamination with salmonella bacteria. This book includes recipes that use raw or lightly cooked eggs, and these should be avoided if you are preparing food for people who fall into these categories.

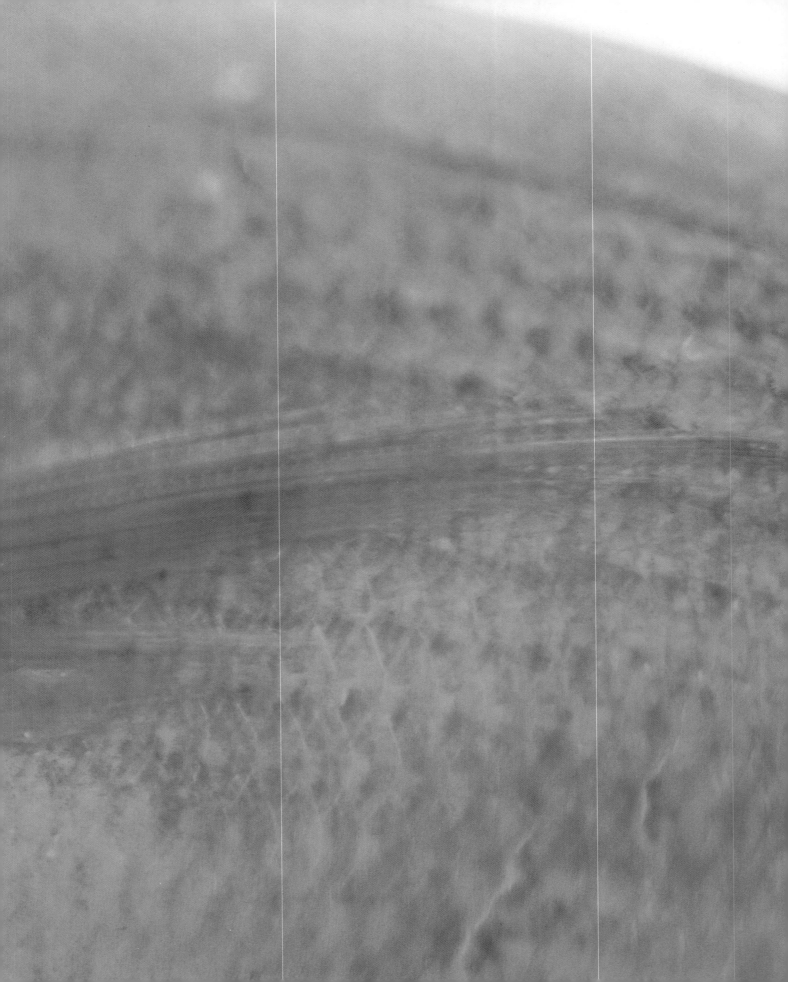

1

buying, preparing and cooking seafood

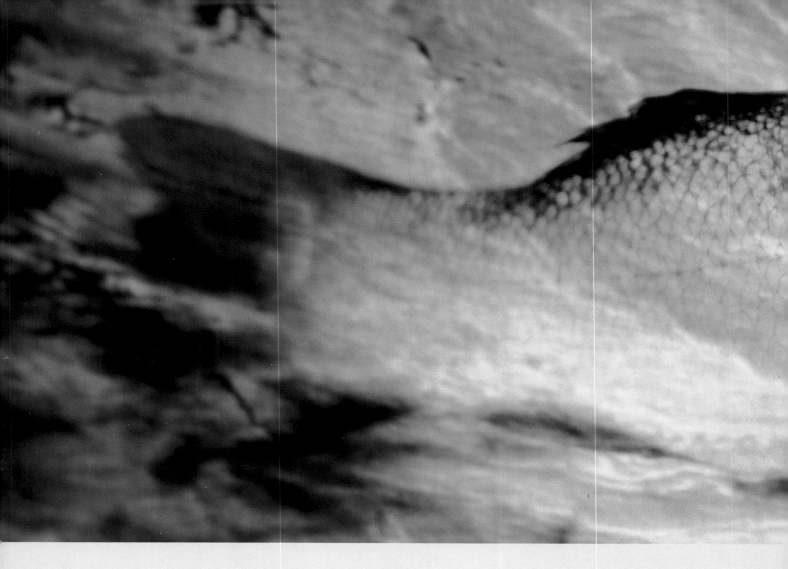

choosing and buying

You're fired with enthusiasm to cook a wonderful fish dish. You walk into a fishmonger's where the counter is brimming with colourful whole fish, creamy white fillets and shellfish – all glistening with freshness. It almost seems a shame to break up the display. But how can you tell if the fish is of a quality to do justice to your cooking? What are the signs you should look for? And, if the fish or the cut you want is not available, what alternative can you buy instead?

I am fortunate in that I have a few trusted suppliers who know the exacting standards I expect. They only send me the very best, because they know I won't put anything but top-quality fish on my menu. Any fish below standard is immediately returned. From time to time, I like to make an early morning visit to the fish

fish and shellfish

market to have a look at what is being landed and sold, and to chat to my favourite suppliers. Not only does it show them that I care and I share their passion for seafood, but it is also because I genuinely love looking at fish – they are such beautiful creatures.

I like to use a great variety of fish in soups, starters, main courses and salads. Each and every species of fish has its own individual characteristics suited to certain styles of dish – full-flavoured and meaty, sweet and tender, or flaky and delicate. You can group fish according to their characteristics, so if one species is not on sale then you can usually find another that has similar traits. For most of the recipes in this book I have suggested alternatives wherever possible.

choosing the best specimens

When buying fish, first look for signs of freshness. The skin, eyes, sheen and general aura of a fresh fish should sparkle and the fish should look as if it is still swimming. The freshest of fish will have a slight covering of mucus on the skin, and it will smell faintly sweet and of the sea, not strong and overtly fishy. Its eyes should look as though they are about to wink, and when you press its flesh it should spring back and feel firm to the touch. If the eyes have started to sink back into their sockets then this is a sign that the flesh is beginning to break down. While the fish may still be edible, it will not taste fresh or at its best. So ask the fishmonger to hold up a sample, and look it closely in the eye.

When it comes to buying ready-prepared, cut and filleted fish there are also a number of signs to look for. The flesh should be firm and, on certain fish such as cod, haddock or salmon, it should not have started to part into flakes. While a slimy mucus may be an indication of freshness on the skin, inside it can be a result of gradual staling. The flesh should look translucent, bright and plump – not dull, limp and lifeless.

varieties and cuts

Often people are daunted by cooking fish because they don't know how to deal with whole fish, or what cuts to buy if the fish has been filleted. At first glance, one white fish fillet tends to look the same as another. It's hard to estimate how many people a whole fish will feed, or whether a thick, chunky fillet will be the same as a longer, thinner one. The best advice I can offer is to ask your fishmonger. Many of them are passionate about fish and only too happy to talk freely. Although high-street fishmongers are dwindling, supermarkets are introducing wet-fish counters in larger stores and the quality is gradually improving.

The shape of a fish determines how it should be filleted and cut. The majority of fish fall into two categories of shape – flat or round. In broad terms, fish can be categorized further, as either white or oily and rich. And beyond this there are those with few bones, which are suitable for cutting into fillets or medallions, and those that are bony with a lot of a flavour – perfect, whole or chopped up, for bouillabaisse.

When the fish is sold boneless, it becomes a fillet. This can be a longer tail end fillet, or one cut across the thicker part of the fish. When a large, round fish is cut across the body into slices, with a central piece of bone and a wrapping of skin, these are called cutlets or steaks.

For pan-roasted fillets, I like to use firm-textured fish that retain their succulence, such as sea bass, halibut, brill, cod and salmon. Red mullet fillets have a more delicate, less chunky texture, but their fuller flavour and attractive skin suit robust, colourful dishes. Of the soles, Dover sole is the most highly revered, but I also like to use a large lemon sole or even very fresh plaice on occasions. The dramatic size and shape

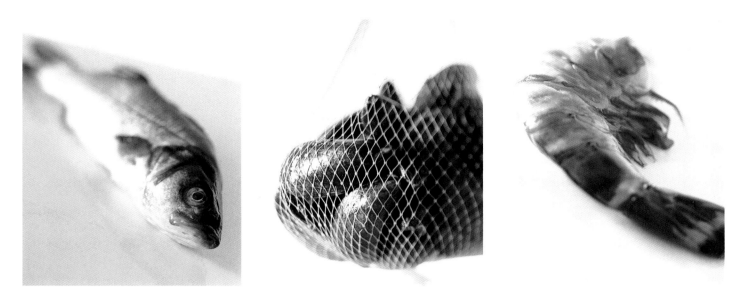

The best advice for cooking fish successfully is to choose very fresh specimens in the first place – with skins or in shells. They should feel plump and firm, or be tightly closed, and have a lightly sweet-salty smell of the bracing open sea.

of skate make it exciting to use – its tender flesh and flavour are a joy to match with punchy ingredients such as capers, tomatoes and anchovies. Fast and efficient refrigerated air transport has meant we now have easier access to warmer-water species of fish such as tuna, snapper and sea bream. These fish are excellent marinated and served in wafer-thin slices as a carpaccio, or used in salads with exotic leaves and dressings. The humbler mackerel, herring and sardine should not be ignored; their richness makes them ideal for grilling or roasting whole until their skins turn crisp.

Some seafood, such as scallops or squid, may be on sale fresh and ready-prepared, but generally these have been frozen and may be quite watery. Shellfish in shells, such as mussels, oysters, scallops and clams, are sold alive and their shells should be tightly closed. Any that are open, even slightly, will be dead or deteriorating rapidly, so check them thoroughly before buying. As wild-fish stocks fluctuate, the farming of fish is increasing. The quality is improving with better, more natural feedstuffs and artificial currents introduced to make the fish swim harder and develop muscle. Farmed salmon, halibut, bass and bream are all on sale, as are certain shellfish, in particular mussels. Oysters have been farmed since Roman days.

A tranquil Scottish loch or Mediterranean cove may be home to thousands of sea creatures. However, the manner of harvesting can affect the quality of fish. For example, scallops that are dredged up in nets may gather sand and debris as they are dragged up. This is not the case with hand-dived scallops, but, naturally, these are more expensive to buy.

different types of fish

When you look through the recipes in this book, you may notice that I use some fish and shellfish more than others. It is not that I think certain fish are superior, but some are more suitable than others for a restaurant kitchen. Fish with a rich flesh, such as salmon, tuna and red mullet, are particularly versatile because their fuller flavour goes well with a great variety of sauces. Cod and halibut are meatier and also more readily available – an important consideration when planning menus. Prawns, lobster and crab have a certain culinary prestige, and look so inviting on a plate with their attractive pink flesh. It helps to know what you are buying, so let's look at some of the different types of seafood available.

anchovy
You can eat anchovies fresh, like sardines, but I tend to use fat, salted fillets. These have tender flesh, and I prefer them to those that have been squashed into a can and feel hard when prised apart. However, canned anchovies are very convenient – just pat them dry to absorb any oil and rinse under cold water.

brill, halibut and turbot
I have grouped these fish together because they are all chunky, flat fish, although their flavours and textures differ slightly. They can be pan-fried, poached, steamed or grilled. Turbot is usually sold cut into steaks, but I prefer to use fillets. You can ask your fishmonger to cut these for you rather than steaks. I use turbot bones to make stock. Halibut can grow to up to 200kg in weight. Found in very cold waters, they have a fine, full flavour. Greenland halibut is not the same as true halibut, nor as fine; chicken halibut is a small fish. Brill is slightly more delicate than turbot, but quite delectable. All three fish are now farmed in cold waters, so the supply and quality is consistent.

cod
Whether shaped into a humble fishcake or a neatly trimmed pavé (square or rectangle), or served with a classic sauce, it is the lovely convex flakes of cod that are perfect. This versatile fish is enjoying a renewed popularity, although once-abundant stocks of cod in the North Atlantic are now under constant threat of overfishing. Certainly the larger fish that once yielded chunky steaks are an increasing rarity. Fishing methods can affect the quality of the flesh: netted or trawled fish can suffer from bruising, whereas the flesh of line-caught cod is undamaged. Buy cod from a good fishmonger and, if possible, buy from a whole fish so you can check that the mottled grey/olive-green skin looks bright and the flesh is firm, not flabby. Ask for fillets, steaks or cutlets. If you see cheaper cod cheeks on sale, use these for stock; the flesh itself is quite soft, and only good for mincing or fishcakes.

eel
Eels are mysterious fish that begin and end their lives in the languid Sargasso Sea, in the middle of the North Atlantic. This is where they are spawned, and it is to here that they return to spawn after a lifespan of about

3 years, during which time they swim into river estuaries. In major fish markets, such as Billingsgate in London, the eels are kept alive in metal drawers. The sight of these eels writhing in the water is almost surreal. Eels are generally skinned as soon as they are killed. For cooking, they can be treated in the same ways as other richly flavoured fish. They are also increasingly available smoked, from specialized eel smokehouses. Smoked eel is delicious served with scrambled eggs or in risotto.

haddock   Like cod, haddock has a meaty, flaky texture and a good flavour. The skin is a rather dull grey with a dark thumbprint mark by the gills. Treat it in the same way as you would cod although, as the whole fish is rarely over 2kg in weight, you will never get as meaty a steak or fillet as you do from a larger cod. If using smoked haddock, buy undyed Finnan haddock, which are whole fish split down the centre, cured and smoked naturally. One useful tip: skin smoked haddock soon after poaching, while still hot, and the skin will peel off more easily. Fish similar to cod and haddock include hake (a fine, greatly underrated fish), whiting, coley/pollock, pollack (a different species) and ling.

john dory   This fish has a skinny, flat body but, unlike a true flat fish, its head is in the right place and not squashed over to one side. John Dory has an enormous head, spooky-looking top spine fins and a low flesh-to-skeleton ratio. You may wonder whether it's worth cooking until you experience its divine taste. In the wild, John Dory is available in the autumn months, but farming in the waters of the Mediterranean has led to a more regular supply. Its name is thought to be based on the French words 'jaune doré' (yellow gold) because of the colour of the skin. The brighter the yellow, the fresher the flesh. This fish has a round, black mark on its side which is traditionally held to be the thumbprint of St Peter.

mackerel and sardine   Although unrelated, both these fish have a beautiful silvery-blue skin, are oily and can be served in the same ways – best pan-fried when very fresh, or grilled whole over barbecue embers. I love cooking baby mackerel, which the French call oisettes; these are best simply fried. Fresh sardines are also wonderful filleted, pan-fried and then dressed lightly in salads. Mackerel and sardines (and pilchards, which are adult sardines) are easily scaled with your fingers under a cold running tap.

monkfish   The firm, smooth, almost milky texture of monkfish is a pleasure to cook. I buy only tails of monkfish: the monster-like head is nearly half the weight of the fish and few fishmongers bother to put it on display. The skin can be a bit tough to pull off the monkfish tails, so ask your fishmonger to oblige. Monkfish is ideal for marinating before cooking (page 40).

red mullet   Good looks, flavour, versatility and a flirtatious look in the eye – red mullet has just about everything going for it. Scale red mullet in a bowl of cold water, rubbing the shiny scales off with your fingers to reveal the prettiest pearl-pink skin. A useful tip when filleting red mullet is to bend the backbone slightly to get a firmer grip. I usually pan-fry the fillets and serve them either hot with a sauce (see the citrus and basil sauce, page 175) or cold as a starter, when they are particularly good partnered with sardines. I sometimes use the liver in a sauce. Red mullet bruise easily, so, whenever possible, buy them from reputable fishmongers.

salmon   The Atlantic salmon is perhaps one of the most popular fish throughout the world. The advent of commercial salmon farming more than 20 years ago has made this king of fish readily available all year round and certainly more affordable. Most people appreciate its full, meaty flavour and firm, flaky texture – even those who claim to dislike fish. Compared side by side, there is a distinct difference between wild and farmed salmon. The former is leaner with a gamier flavour, and is available only during the summer months. My supplier is able to obtain a superior farmed fish which is fed on a diet closer to that found in the wild. The fish are also reared in spacious pens, with currents that encourage them to swim and develop muscle. Consequently the flesh is not fatty or pale, although I always prefer to use the denser loin part of the fish rather than the fattier belly. When you buy salmon, choose the middle cuts if you want a thicker fillet. That way there is less risk of overcooking and ending up with a chewy texture.

sea bass   A few years ago, my signature dish was a tranche of sea bass with a crisp, lightly browned skin served with a whisked vanilla-scented velouté. I still love to cook this aristocrat of the sea, with its beautiful shimmering silver skin, and it is equally good poached or steamed. Sea bass is perhaps one of the most expensive of fish – often twice the price of cod – but it seems to be liked by everyone. The best is wild and line-caught, but satisfying the great demand has led to bass farming, especially in the Mediterranean.

sea bream   Breams exist in a variety of shapes, sizes, colours and names. To add to the confusion, menus often refer to the fish by their French names. So let me explain what I mean when I refer to breams. My star is the royal bream, which we call dorade royale, also known as the gilt-head bream. Red bream are called daurade (or dorade) by the French, while the bream loved by Oriental chefs is the black bream or dorade grise. Farming of dorade royale has meant that supplies are now more certain. As with many other fish, breams need to be scaled before cooking. Use the back of a knife, scraping from tail to head, and rinse frequently.

skate   In general only the skate wings are sold, skinned and ready to cook. Skate have cartilage but no bones. The flesh comes away in long strands, and is tender and delicious. Serve skate grilled on the bone with butter and lemon juice, or try the moulds on page 97.

snapper	The word snapper seems to be used quite loosely by fishmongers for any pretty pink-skinned fish flown in from tropical climes. However, as they are all cooked and served in similar ways, maybe it doesn't matter too much. Other names you will come across for snapper are bourgeois, capitaine and emperor. Snapper provide really good eating and their rich, meaty flesh goes well with punchy-flavoured sauces, making them perfect for party dishes.
sole and plaice	These popular flat fish are the mainstays of British fish cooking. The very best is the superb Dover sole. Unfortunately, the price of Dover sole is becoming prohibitive, and most stocks are diverted to the restaurant trade. Lemon sole, which has the distinction of the same name in several languages, is considerably cheaper and a favourite of mine. Sole tastes best if it is allowed to 'relax' a little before cooking – some say up to 3 days after catching is ideal – because if cooked too fresh the flesh can be slightly tough. Plaice can be disappointingly bland, and young specimens can be very thin, with more skin and bones than flesh. Very bright yellow spots on the skin are a good indicator of freshness.
sturgeon	I include this fish as something of a curiosity, but it is well worth trying if you find it on sale in the local fishmonger's. In its whole glory, sturgeon looks quite primeval, with a hard, almost leathery skin and beautiful geometric fins on top. The flesh is quite rich and tastes a little like catfish.
trout	Trout are bony fish with a moist pink flesh that is best suited to simple cooking methods such as grilling and pan-roasting. The opportunities for eating trout fresh from the stream are becoming increasingly rare – most trout on sale are specially reared on fish farms. However, as a result, trout is always easy to obtain and is generally very fresh. The freshest trout still have a slimy mucus on their skins. If you are lucky enough to obtain trout straight from the net, they are best cooked au bleu – fried in a hot, seasoned pan with just a little oil, then finished with a knob of butter and a squeeze of lemon.
tuna	Tuna is a popular fish in Mediterranean, Japanese, American and Australian kitchens. There are many different species. I buy line-caught bluefin (the best) or sometimes yellowfin. Fresh tuna will invariably be on display in whole loins from which steaks are cut. Parts of the loin will have visible blood lines running through – try to avoid these. A good tuna steak is almost the colour of spring lamb and the flesh is firm and meaty. Tuna is a very rich fish, needing little additional oil. It has a dense texture, so don't overcook it or it will become dry like overcooked steak. In Japan, sashimi is made from wafer-thin slices of raw tuna, using fish that is exceptionally fresh. If you find a fishmonger that sells to ex-patriot Japanese, join the queue and buy your tuna there. Steer clear of buying thawed-out tuna steaks – they seem to weep.

shellfish and other seafood

molluscs: oyster, mussel and clam

There are two main species of oyster: natives or flats (belons in French) and the Pacific rock oysters. Oysters are priced according to size. British and French numbering systems differ slightly. British No.1s are the biggest, with a weight of 120g or more, down to No.5s at around 55g. French oyster classification also involves descriptions: fines, speciales and claires (fattened for colour and flavour). Numbering starts at 000 (UK No.1) through 00, 0, 1, 2 and 3.

Mussels are best bought farmed, simply because they are grown on ropes in clear and tranquil estuaries and are therefore cleaner and plumper than wild varieties. Irish mussels are particularly good. Buy them bagged and alive, that is with their shells tightly closed. Clams come in an immense variety of shapes and sizes (sometimes you can even buy fresh razor-shell clams in supermarkets). I tend to use them only in soups or risottos, not having the abundant selection found in North America. Mussels and clams are wonderful steamed together on a bed of seaweed in the French coquillage.

crustaceans: crab, lobster, prawn and scallop

I buy crustaceans alive from suppliers around the coasts of Britain. The best lobsters, scallops and langoustines are to be found in the clear, cold waters of Scotland, although very occasionally I will use Canadian lobsters if homegrown species are scarce. The reason I buy live shellfish is because the flesh spoils quickly once they are killed. My methods are quick and humane (see pages 35–36). Always buy shellfish that are heavy for their size; the actual shell can account for more than three-quarters of the weight (you can use the shells to make stock). Fresh lobsters and crabs are sold with their claws bound in elastic bands to stop them attacking not only humans but also each other. They are best bought before they start to shed their old shells, so be aware of barnacles and well-worn claws. The males may have larger claws, but the females are believed to have sweeter flesh. Prices are most reasonable in the summer months.

If you can only buy ready-cooked lobsters and crabs, then make sure their bodies, claws and legs are well curled under, as this indicates they were in good condition when killed. Lobsters are often missing one claw, and sometimes both. This is not caused by careless handling, rather by lobsters fighting with each other. The main body flesh will still be in perfect condition.

I like to use the very best king scallops (the true Coquille St Jacques), hand-dived from the west coast of Scotland, and I open them myself. It really does pay to buy the freshest and best quality you can. Previously frozen scallops weep in the pan. Why pay money for water?

squid

I prefer to use baby squid because they are the most tender. Again my supplies (the common European species) are home-caught, although imported supplies can be good, especially from the Falkland Islands, which technically still makes them British.

caviar

It may be the ultimate luxury food, but caviar is being eaten by more and more people, many of whom want to know more about how to choose and use it. If you are going to spend a lot of money, then it makes sense to understand how to spend it wisely.

Caviar is the roe of the sturgeon and is simply salted for preservation and then packed. After salting, the caviar may be sold fresh, as it is, or it may be pasteurized or vacuum-packed for longer storage. The finest caviar is obtained from sturgeon from the landlocked Caspian Sea, which is some 1500km long, bordering Russia in the north where the waters are chilly down to the warmer shores of Iran in the south. I only buy Caspian caviar, fished, preserved and packed in Iran. Government regulations are more stringent and agents are specially selected. My agent, Ramin Rohgar of Imperial Caviar UK, has become a close friend and knows my requirements so well now that he suggests the best qualities to suit the dishes I serve.

There are four main varieties of caviar and their value depends mainly on rarity. Caviar is only taken from mature fish at least 10 years old – some sturgeon can reach 100 years of age. Once caught, the fish cannot be returned to the water to grow more roe.

Top of the rarity stakes is Beluga caviar with its delicate texture, silver-grey colour and creamy, almost buttery taste. Imperial caviar, produced only by albino Caraburun sturgeon is a brilliant gold colour and has a mild, nutty flavour. Osietra is popular with caviar aficionados for its firm and nutty texture (it is especially good for serving as a garnish). Sevruga is the most widely available variety of caviar, and the one I tend to use in dishes and sauces.

Caviar is very delicate and sensitive to a rise in temperature, and you should only buy from a reliable agent to guarantee a high quality. Check the individual caviar eggs are not bruised or oily, and, once opened, keep the tin well chilled and consume within a few days.

I like to use caviar in a variety of sauces, stirring it in just before serving (see Spaghetti with Caviar and Crème Fraîche, page 137); folded into whipped crème fraîche (wonderful as a filling for baby new potatoes for canapés); or shaped as tiny quenelles (page 219) for a garnish.

calculating quantities

In the restaurant, my dishes tend to be light and the portions precise. I do not believe in loading up plates with food. As all our fish is served neatly filleted and trimmed, we can be quite exact on calculating quantities. With shellfish you can normally go by numbers.

fish

whole fish When you buy a large whole fish, gutted but with the head left on, expect to lose around half of the weight through filleting and skinning. Smaller whole fish, such as a trout or a small sea bass, weigh 300–400g, and one fish is enough per person. For flat fish, such as sole, allow one 300–340g whole fish per person.

filleted fish For firm white fish, allow 120–150g of trimmed weight per person. If you are buying fish filleted, with skin on, the skin will make up just under one-quarter of the weight. So a 150g piece will weigh about 120g after skinning. A 500g piece of fish will serve 4 people. When serving richer fish, such as tuna or salmon, allow slightly less per head. For thinly sliced smoked salmon or gravalax, allow around 100g per head.

shellfish and other seafood

langoustine I generally allow 5 for a starter, but if you are using smaller Atlantic prawns, you will need 10–12 per person.

lobster A lobster at around 700g in its shell will feed 2 for a starter, one at 400–500g will provide one main course.

mussel These are sold by weight or capacity: 500g (equivalent to about a pint in old measures) yields around 16 mussels, which is the right amount for one person; a quart bag should be enough for 2 people.

scallop Allow 3 per person for a starter and 4–5 per head for a main course.

oyster I usually serve oysters in half dozens, although if dipped in batter as beignets I allow 4 per person.

sea urchin Allow 3–4 per head.

squid An unprepared squid weighing 175g serves one person as a starter. As a main course allow 2 the same size or a larger one of about 300g per person.

caviar Allow 25–30g, depending on your budget.

equipment

Most of the fish that comes into my kitchen is whole, fresh and glistening. This means it is possible to check the gills, eyes and skin thoroughly before preparation begins. Raw fish flesh is soft and easily damaged, while shellfish can be difficult to clean and handle, so specific utensils and equipment are essential for their preparation. Razor-sharp knives are vital for cutting through the soft flesh, leaving neat cut edges, and for removing the skin quickly and cleanly. Skill and technique are needed to prepare fish, not heavy-handedness. For example, when it comes to producing a neat skinless fillet, holding the knife at the correct angle is far more important than putting pressure on the blade.

knives
A glance through my knife collection reveals a variety of lengths, shapes and sizes, from 25cm long, thin, bendy cook's knives, to sturdy 5cm oyster knives. Apart from those used for cutting open hard shells, most of the knives you use should be quite pliable, which will enable them to be lightly bent to just the right angle to sweep between skin and flesh. When you buy a knife for filleting, press the blade on a hard surface to flex it, removing it from the packaging if necessary. Make sure the handle is comfortable to hold and fits your hand. A heavy-bladed cook's knife has many uses, including chopping through bones and, used upside-down, de-scaling fish.

knife steel
Regularly sharpen all your knives with a steel. Before you skin, fillet or bone a fish, rub each side of the knife you are going to use up and down on the steel a dozen times or so. You should do this every time – it only takes seconds. In addition, depending on how much you use your knives, treat them to an occasional re-grinding. You can arrange this through your fishmonger or butcher as they have their knives serviced by a knife grinder about once a fortnight.

chopping board
A large wooden or plastic board is essential. Before chopping, lay the board on top of a clean, damp cloth to stop it slipping. Wash the board thoroughly between uses by first scrubbing with cold running water to remove fishy odours, then scrubbing well in hot, soapy water. Rinse, dry well and stand it up against a wall to air. This is not only more hygienic, but prevents fishy smells lingering.

scaler
Many fish have scales that can be removed easily with your fingers under cold running water, but others need more aggressive treatment. For these, I use the back of a heavy-duty knife, rubbing from the tail end to the head. Before you begin, put the fish in a large bin bag and work inside the bag to stop the scales from flying everywhere. If you prepare a lot of fresh fish, it may be worth investing in a proper fish scaler. Fish that need to be scaled in this way include the breams and snapper.

tweezers or pliers	Some fish have tiny pin bones in their flesh that are not removed when the fish is boned. By running your fingertips along a fillet, against the grain of the flesh, you can feel for the thin bone tips. If the flesh is soft you can sometimes pull the bones out with your fingernails, otherwise use a pair of large tweezers or small pliers to extract the bones.
craft knife	Chefs have very sharp knives – sharper than mortals do, so for scoring the skin of fish at home I recommend that you use a razor-sharp craft knife or scalpel.
larding needle	Occasionally a recipe calls for strips of a fish such as salmon to be threaded through firm white fish – a technique known as larding. To do this you will need a long larding needle with a hook or clasp at one end for fixing on a strip of fish.
pans and steamers	A heavy-based sauté or frying pan is essential for even browning. Ideally choose one with a metal handle so you can put it in the oven for a few minutes to finish pan-roasting. A heavy, ridged, cast-iron grill pan is perfect for grilling chunky fish steaks or fillets. A fish kettle is useful for poaching large whole fish, such as salmon, although wrapping in foil and baking is just as effective. A large metal steamer is useful, or use bamboo baskets that stack one on top of another. These are available from Oriental supermarkets and are cheap, effective and last for many years. Make sure they fit over your largest saucepan.
other equipment	In addition to specific utensils and equipment, you will need other items for preparing fish dishes, such as a powerful food processor to purée fish flesh, chinois sieves for straining stocks and sauces, a drum sieve with a scraper for rubbing through raw fish to make fine mousselines, tongs for turning fish when grilling or deep-frying, and, of course, a flexible fish slice.

A well-equipped fish cook will have (clockwise from the top): skimmer, fish slice, slotted spoon, large spoon, ladle, lobster crackers, kitchen string, bamboo steaming baskets, mortar and pestle, knives, knife steel, 2 kinds of pliers, oyster knife, frying and sauté pans, chinois sieve, all on a cutting board.

preparing fish

Twice a day, fish and shellfish are delivered to my kitchens, neatly boxed but still whole, as the freshness and quality of the seafood are easier to gauge this way, and I prefer to fillet and prepare it myself. Consequently, my chefs and I have become as deft at filleting and trimming fish – and at prising open shellfish – as the most experienced fishmongers.

Preparing and filleting fish requires a certain amount of skill and precision. These tasks become easier with practice, but to get started it helps to have a basic knowledge of the bone structures of round and flat fish and of the internal 'layout' of shellfish. Most fish have a central backbone, but not all of them have long 'ribs'. In round fish the backbone runs along the top of the fish with the fins astride. Flat fish are merely round

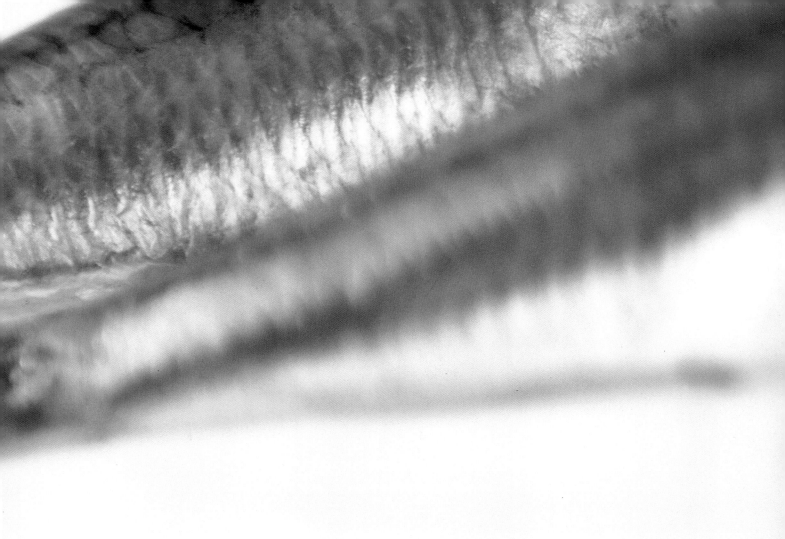

and **shellfish**

fish that look as if they have been flattened, so the backbone runs down the centre. Conveniently the skin markings indicate where the central bone is located, so you can work out where to make the first cut when filleting – just below the head. When preparing fish, the scaling should be done first, followed by filleting, pin boning and then skinning and trimming.

    To prepare shellfish for cooking or for eating raw, the shells should first be scrubbed clean if necessary. Clams, oysters and scallops are then snapped open before removing any innards. The juices from raw oysters – as well as those trapped inside cooked mussels, lobsters and crabs – should be reserved for adding to sauces and stocks. Fishbones and shells can be saved for making stock (pages 58–59).

The first step in preparing your fish is to scale it, if necessary (or ask your fishmonger to do it for you). Before you begin filleting, have the correct equipment ready: a thin-bladed 20cm filleting knife (sharpened with a knife steel) and a large, heavy chopping board, placed on top of a damp cloth to hold it steady.

preparing fish

filleting round fish

You get two large half fillets from a round fish. Some books tell you to gut the fish first, but I prefer to leave the guts in so that the fish remains firm to work on. I fillet one side first, then gut before turning over to fillet the second side. Leave the head on whilst filleting. If the fish is small, such as a mullet or mackerel, bend it round slightly to tighten the flesh, making it easier to cut.

1   Lay the fish on its side and make a diagonal cut behind the head. With the tail end towards you, make an incision into the skin down one side of the backbone, cutting from head to tail. Start to cut away the fillet in small, sweeping strokes. You should be able to hear the knife scraping against the bones.
2   When you get to the tail end, turn the fish over and repeat the process to remove the fillet on the other side.

filleting flat fish

A large flat fish will give you four quarter fillets – two from each side. However, very large fish, such as turbot, will yield many more portions.

1   Cut around the head and gills first, without removing them. Check for the line on the skin that runs down the centre of the fish and corresponds to the backbone. Starting at the head end, use the tip of the knife to cut through the flesh to the rib bones down one side of the backbone to the tail.
2   Cut the flesh away in short strokes, scraping the blade of the knife against the bones. Turn the fish around and remove the quarter fillet on the other side of the backbone, starting at the tail end this time. Turn the fish over and repeat the process on the other side. Flat fish do not have pin bones, but you will need to trim away the fin bones from the sides of the fillets.

filleting salmon

The soft flesh of salmon can break apart if it is overhandled. Because of this, we fillet whole salmon from one side only, which means there is no need to turn the fish over for the second fillet.

1   Start by filleting one side of the salmon in the same way as for other round fish.·
2   Instead of turning over the half-filleted fish, open it flat like a book and cut out the skeleton from the top side.

chunky medallions (I usually do this after cooking); trimmed into neat steaks; or laid head to tail in opposite directions, tied together with kitchen string and roasted in the oven like a joint.

1   Using a sharp knife with a short blade, slice off the thin grey membrane, lifting it up as you cut. Take care not to cut into the flesh beneath.
2   Using a sharp filleting knife, cut the flesh from the central bone into two long fillets.

skinning fish

Not all fish are the same, and over the years experience has taught me that you have to take account of their differences. Red mullet, for example, has to be scaled in a bowl of cold water using your fingers because the scales are soft and the delicate pink skin is easily damaged. Halibut and sturgeon have a tougher skin than red mullet, being leathery and hard to cut, but the flesh is softer and the bones are thinner. Sea bass has a delicate flesh, and both bass and mullet have backbones that can separate out, causing the knife to slip through. I prefer to skin all fillets just above the 'blood line' – the thin, dark brown layer between skin and flesh.

Place the fillet skin side down on the chopping board, tail end towards you. At the tail end, make a small cut through the flesh to the skin, and take hold of the skin at the tail end with the fingers of the other hand. Holding the knife with the blade at a 45 degree angle between flesh and skin, work it up a little towards the other end until there is enough skin to grasp firmly. Work the knife from side to side under the flesh and just above the skin towards the head end. Trim the fillet around the sides to neaten it.

preparing monkfish

Monkfish are usually sold just as tails. They are easy to fillet, having just one central bone which can be removed with the tip of a sharp knife. Often the fishmonger will sell monkfish skinned, but you will have to remove the grey, slightly elastic membrane that clings to the flesh (otherwise the fillets will curl up during cooking). Before cooking I wrap the fillets tightly in cling film and chill overnight to firm them. The prepared fillets can then be cut into

trimming fish for cooking

There are few things better than a beautiful fresh fish cooked simply on or off the bone in all its natural glory. But I also find a great deal of pleasure in trimming fish into neat shapes. Trimmed fish not only looks better, but also cooks more evenly. While it may seem wasteful to cut away a fin edge, it does mean that the thickest part of a fillet can cook to perfection. The trimmings are reserved for use elsewhere. Nothing is wasted in my kitchen. Once the fish has been filleted, checked for pin bones and skinned, it can be cut into neat shapes such as rectangular tranches, medallions or diamonds.

Salmon, sea bass, turbot and halibut can be cut into neat tranches, each weighing about 120g. If the tranches are left with skin on, score this so that it cooks crisply and attractively. Mullet fillets can be scored more casually, about three or four times. For steaming tranches of fish, wrap them first in cling film, then chill to 'set' the flesh. The same is true of monkfish fillets, especially if you intend to roast small whole monkfish tails. You can also trim a mixture of different fish fillets into small diamonds and serve them as a medley of fish.

1   Using the tip of a sharp knife, cut through the 'frilly' edges of the fish fillets to give a neat shape.

2   To score the skin of a fish for an attractive crispy appearance, take the tip of a sharp knife, scalpel or craft knife and make cuts in the skin evenly and closely, leaving a small border.

pin boning

A perfectly skinned fillet of fish can be spoilt by unexpected pin bones, so it is important to pull them all out as carefully as possible.

Feel for pin bones by running the tips of your fingers smoothly along the length of a fillet, working against the grain. Use your fingernails, tweezers or a pair of pliers to remove any bones that you find.

Preparing shellfish yourself rather than asking your fishmonger to do it ensures that it is at the peak of freshness and full of flavour. There is no need to be nervous about undertaking this task at home because, as with filleting fish, it becomes easier with practice.

preparing shellfish

scallops

Hand-dived scallops are cleaner and plumper than mechanically dredged ones. Any scallops with shells that have already opened will be dead and their freshness uncertain.

1   For safety's sake, you may wish to wrap your supporting hand in a towel or cloth. Insert a short, heavy-bladed knife between the shells near the hinge muscle and push up sharply to break the hinge. Snap off the flat shell and then discard it.

2   You will see the skirt, an orange coral (the roe), some black innards and a large pearly-white muscle. Work the knife underneath the skirt (which may be sandy) and gently lift it up, easing off all the soft tissue and detaching the small muscle where it joins the shell. Discard the skirt and black innards.

3   I use the main white muscle and discard the smaller, firmer muscle. However, this small muscle is perfectly edible so you may not want to waste it

and you can use it to flavour stocks or sauces. I also tend to remove the coral, but, again, this can be eaten if you wish. (Sometimes, I dry out the coral overnight in a very low oven until brittle, and then grind it to a powder to use as a flavouring for sauces and risottos.)

Wash each scallop well and pat dry with kitchen paper towels, then stack upright to hold the shape; cover with cling film. Chill for 24 hours to allow the flesh to firm and any excess moisture to dry out a little. Really fresh scallops can be kept chilled for a good two days.

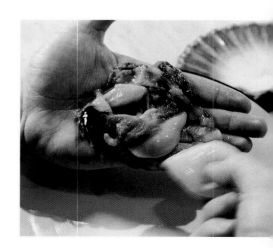

oysters

The types of oyster most widely available are native (or belon) and rock (or Pacific) oysters. Native oysters have smoother shells and are a little harder to open, so it is perhaps better to start with the craggier rock oysters. You will need a small, sharp oyster knife and a thick, clean cloth or towel to prepare them. Always discard any oysters whose shells have already opened. When you shell the oysters, work over a bowl so that you can save the juices to use in a soup or sauce.

To serve fresh oysters in the shell, simply flip the oysters over to present the rounded side uppermost, and serve the shells nestling on crushed ice or mounds of rock salt. If you intend to poach the oysters or make beignets (page 107), store them in their juices in a plastic container in the refrigerator and use within a few hours.

1   Hold the oyster firmly, rounded side down. Wrap your thumb – or your whole hand if you prefer – in a cloth or towel. Using an oyster knife, slowly but firmly push the tip of the blade through the edge of the top hinge between the shells. Don't jab at it, as you will get pieces of shell in the oyster. As soon as the hinge snaps, pull up the top shell, saving the juices in the lower shell. Cut through the muscle attached to the top shell and discard the top shell.

2   Slide the knife under the oyster to cut through the muscle that attaches it to the bottom shell. Check you have not dropped any tiny pieces of shell inside and scrape off any foam, if necessary. Never wash oysters in water, as this will diminish the flavour. If you need to rinse away any fragments of shell or grit, do so using the oyster juices.

cockles and mussels

Fresh cockles appear sporadically in fishmonger's, whereas mussels are widely available, often sold in net bags. Unlike scallops and oysters, both cockles and mussels are steamed open and shelled after cooking.

Check for any wispy 'beards' (thread-like strands on the shells) and pull these off with your fingers. Scrub well under cold running water, discarding any that have opened or have cracked or broken shells. Cook according to your recipe or for a few minutes in a little white wine flavoured with onion and herbs. The shells should open once they are cooked. Discard any shells that have failed to open. Unless you are serving them on the shell, snap off one half of the shells and pull out the cooked cockles or mussels. Retain the cooking liquor and use to complete the recipe.

prawns, langoustines and crayfish

Although these vary in size, they are similar in shape and can all be prepared in the same way. (Langoustines are also known as Dublin Bay prawns.)

1   Pull the heads from the bodies and discard (or you can save the heads with the shells for making stock, if you wish). Pull off the legs and peel off the shells. Squeezing the body shell of a prawn before peeling loosens it and makes it easier to peel off. Langoustines and crayfish, which have harder shells than prawns, may need to have the underside of the shell cut open before it can be peeled off. In this case, use scissors to snip the shell.

2   Larger prawns and langoustines have a dark intestinal vein running down the back which you should remove with the tip of a sharp knife. If the vein is hard to see, peel back a little of the flesh until it is revealed. Pat the prepared shellfish dry with kitchen paper and stack neatly together in a small container, covered in cling film. Keep in the refrigerator until you are ready to use it.

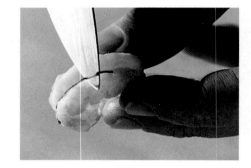

lobsters

Several of the recipes in this book call for cooked lobster, which you can buy from your fishmonger. Even better, you may be able to find large ready-cooked lobster tails. However, there may be occasions when you need to cook a live lobster, and preparing one for the first time can be daunting. There are humane methods to ensure the least possible distress is caused. When you buy a lobster, make sure it feels heavy in relation to the size of its shell. Hen lobsters are preferable. Make sure the claws are secured with strong elastic bands, and that you handle the lobster with determined firmness.

Animal welfare groups suggest you make the lobster feel sleepy before killing it, by placing it in a freezer at -20°C for about 2 hours (that is, with the fast-freeze switch on). The lobster will start to hibernate and can then be dispatched humanely. Wrap it in a towel and place it belly side down on a board. On the back of the head you will see a cross. Quickly and firmly push the tip of a large, sharp knife into it, to kill the lobster instantly.

1   To prepare both raw and cooked lobsters, either pull the head from the body and use just the tail meat and claws, or, if preparing a whole lobster, split the shell in two down the centre.

Remove the small stomach sac and intestine, and discard. Take out the greenish tomalley (the liver) and the green coral (the roe). Both of these can be used in sauces. Langoustines dipped in lobster coral and pan-fried turn the most glorious orangey-pink colour. If you can't use the coral immediately, just freeze it in a small pot for another time. Pull off the claws.

2   To remove the flesh from cooked lobster claws, first snap back the top pincer of the claw, then pull out the translucent 'bone'. Use a sharp, heavy-bladed knife to crack the top of each claw, then twist the knife slightly to break the claw in two. The flesh can then be pulled out in one piece. Reserve the shells for stock. If the lobster is uncooked, first blanch the claws and shells for about 30 seconds in boiling water or court-bouillon. Remove and leave until cool enough to handle. The flesh will then be easier to remove.

crabs

If bought live, check the claws are tied securely with strong bands, then kill and cook the crab before preparation. If you have to kill it yourself, pierce the main nerves behind the eyes, then plunge into boiling water or court-bouillon. Allow 15 minutes per 500g. Remove and cool. (A 1.5kg crab will yield 285g white meat and 130g brown meat.)

1 · Lay the crab on its back and twist off the legs and claws. Hold the rough, pale belly shell just by the eyes and pull – it should come off in one piece. If necessary, thump the front of the crab firmly on a board to loosen the body shell. Inside you will see a small sac and long, hairy grey 'fingers' (the gills). Pull these off and discard. Scrape the meat out of the body shell and claws, keeping the brown and white meat separate. Brown meat is soft, almost runny; white meat is fibrous with a pink hue.

2   If the smaller claws are large enough, you can pick out the meat with a skewer or trussing needle.

3   Cut the pale belly shell in half and use a long, thin skewer to pull out as much white meat as you can find, cracking the shell each time you come to another cavity. Crack open the claws (the two large and the several smaller ones) by tapping with a small hammer and pull out the meat with a skewer. If you want to serve the crab meat in the body shell, neaten it by using a small hammer to tap along the faint line visible around the underside of the shell.

sea urchins

If you ever manage to get hold of sea urchins, you'll find that they are quite easy to prepare. The part eaten is the soft, coral-coloured tongues inside. These can be eaten raw or used to flavour butter (page 74), which can be melted into scrambled eggs or pasta, or added to a velouté sauce.

1 Hold the urchin with the circular beak uppermost. Using kitchen scissors, push the tip into the shell and cut around the beak. Pull out the beak and discard, then drain off any juices.

2 You should be able to see several orange corals or tongues inside the sea urchin. Using the handle of a teaspoon, gently pull out the soft tongues and tip them on to a plate. Clean the tongues with the tip of a knife, removing any dark materials.

squid

What may appear daunting at first is actually quite simple to tackle. Squid consist of two main parts: the head and tentacles, and the body sac. If you have a number of squid with ink sacs, freeze the sacs to use in risottos or sauces.

1   First pull the head with the adjoining tentacles away from the body. Cut the tentacles off in one piece just below the eyes. Discard the head.

2   The side 'flaps' on the body are edible, so you may like to pull them off first. We discard them at the restaurant, however. Pull out the inner transparent tube (pen), the soft white tissue (roe) and the silvery-grey ink sac and discard. Wash the inside of the body tube and rub off the dark skin with your fingers under cold running water. The tube can be left whole and stuffed, or sliced into rings. The tentacles should be used too.

There are no hard and fast rules about matching fish with herbs and spices. In fact, full-flavoured and firm-textured fish simply cry out for a whole range of innovative combinations of flavourings. Bear in mind that some fish, such as plaice or turbot, only require a hint of spice and lighter herbs to do their delicate, subtle flavours justice. A little knowledge will prevent expensive errors.

herbs and spices for fish

herbs

Herbs and spices add colour and visual interest as well as flavour to fish. Some spices turn the flesh a pale golden hue, while sprigs and leaves of aromatic herbs can be layered between fillets or inserted into whole fish to add contrasting colour. Parsley, chervil, chives and tarragon are perhaps the classic fish herbs, used not just for flavouring but also as dainty garnishes. They often form a core around which I will flavour a sauce or dressing. For example, I like to braise fillets of turbot with a simple mixture of fresh chervil and chives.

Basil is another favourite of mine. I like to deep-fry the baby leaves as a garnish. Sometimes I wrap rosemary tips in the larger leaves and use them to spike chunky fillets of cod. I do the same with thyme sprigs, wrapping them in sage leaves and pushing them into monkfish or whole baby turbot. Both fish flavoured in this way make wonderful barbecue dishes. For a different type of flavouring, I crush lemon grass stalks and infuse them in oil for vinaigrette to serve with lobster or large prawns.

Bay is a favourite stockpot herb in my bouquet garni, along with thyme, parsley stalks, celery and leek, plus sometimes herb fennel.

Making a fresh bouquet garni

You can make a simple bouquet garni by tying a bunch of fresh herbs together with kitchen string. Alternatively, try this method which uses the 'butt' of a large leek – the two outer leaves of the vegetable – as a wrapping for the herbs.

1 large leek
½ small celery stick
1 sprig fresh thyme
few parsley stalks
1 bay leaf
½ tsp black peppercorns
½ tsp white peppercorns
6 coriander seeds
kitchen string for tying

Peel off the two outer leaves of the leek and spread out in a double layer. Save the inner part for another use. Place the celery, thyme, parsley stalks and bay leaf inside the leek leaves. Spoon in the peppercorns and coriander seeds. Fold in the ends and sides of the leek and roll into a neat parcel. Wind kitchen string around the parcel and tie to secure.

spices

I tend to use aromatic flavourings without the fiery heat of chillies, such as a little ginger juice, a pretty star anise, a teaspoon of coriander seeds, or a pinch of mild curry powder or five-spice powder. My particular favourite is a saffron seasoning. Simply chop or crush some good-quality saffron strands (Spanish preferably) and mix with fine sea salt. Sprinkle this on to fish just before pan-frying. It not only flavours the fish, but colours it too. Try it with fillets of red mullet to produce a stunning contrast of pink skin and golden flesh.

A selection of whole spices can be mixed and stored in a peppermill for adding zest quickly to a fish dish. Here are 2 mixes to try.

Chinese pepper mix

Yellow mustard seeds are hot, so use them with caution according to taste. This spicy mix is especially good with tuna, and is an essential element of Spice-Crusted Tuna with Chicory Salad on page 184.

30g allspice berries
30g yellow mustard seeds
30g black mustard seeds
30g Sichuan red peppercorns

Aromatic pepper mix

This all-purpose spice mix should prove a useful addition to your dry store cupboard. It is very good to use with meat as well as fish.

30g white peppercorns
30g black peppercorns
20g coriander seeds
3 star anise, broken into pieces
1 tbsp fennel seeds
1 tsp whole cloves
½ nutmeg, grated

marinating

I marinate fish for several reasons, but certainly not to tenderize tough flesh. Fish doesn't need it. The main purpose of marinating is to add flavour. Even a few minutes in a light marinade imparts the essence of oils, herbs or spices to the flesh. Marinating also relaxes the texture of a fish and helps to extract water, thus making the flesh easier to roast. This is certainly true of monkfish and of squid, which I score first in a criss-cross pattern. Finally, marinating extends the storage life of fish.

Basic marinade

200ml good-quality olive oil
1 tsp coriander seeds, lightly crushed
4 thin strips lemon or lime zest
1 bay leaf

1 sprig fresh rosemary
1 sprig fresh tarragon
1 sprig fresh thyme or lemon thyme
1 tsp lime juice
1 tsp balsamic vinegar
1 tbsp Aromatic Pepper Mix (left), coarsely ground

Note that there is no salt added at this stage. You can season the fish just before cooking. For variation, you could also add any of the following ingredients: lightly crushed pink peppercorns; a good pinch of crushed saffron strands; fresh lemon grass, crushed and infused in a little heated oil; or sherry vinegar instead of balsamic vinegar.

Fish suitable for marinating

Red mullet, monkfish, salmon, sardines, mackerel, dorade grise (black bream), dorade royale (gilt-head bream), tuna, scallops, squid, cuttlefish, John Dory, langoustines and lobster all taste excellent when they are marinated before cooking.

Different types of fish and seafood can be marinated for different lengths of time, but in general most can be left for 1–2 days. All fish should be filleted and trimmed beforehand, then placed in a flat dish or other suitable container, covered with cling film and left to marinate in the fridge. If the fridge is crowded, you might find marinating in a heavy polythene food bag, tied securely with a wire tie, will take up less space.

Cooking marinated fish

Marinated fish is much easier to handle than raw fish and you will find that cooking times can be reduced by about one-third. It is also easier to identify the 'cuisson' (see page 44). To pan-fry fish that has been marinated, preheat a non-stick frying pan until a good steady heat rises off it (hold your hand flat over the pan, at a safe distance, to test this). There is no need to add oil because there will be enough in the marinade to prevent the fish from sticking.

cooking

Fish is the ultimate quick-cook food. Cooking times are measured in minutes rather than hours and, once fish is cooked, it will be tender. There is no need to carry on with long, slow cooking to soften tough fibres, as is the case with meat. (The only exception is squid, but more of that later.) There are several basic techniques for cooking fish, and I have outlined the seven methods I use the most in the following pages. All of them are quick and simple, and ensure that the fish remains moist and tender. Where appropriate, I have indicated the best varieties of fish for each method.

fish **simply**

Pan-roasting, a combination of cooking on the hob and in the oven, produces succulent fillets of fish with a deliciously caramelized surface. For braising, flavoured liquid is added for the oven stage, to create a rich, glossy sauce. Grilling can be done on a ridged grill pan or under a top-heat grill, or outdoors over hot coals, marinating or basting the fish to give juicy results. Poaching retains the natural fish flavours, as do steaming and microwaving, and with all three of these simple cooking methods the fish turns out moist and tender. In contrast, fish deep-fried in batter or an egg-and-crumb coating is crisp and quite irresistible.

The point at which fish is cooked is often called the cuisson by chefs – that is, when it is just ready but not overcooked. Looking for the cuisson is easy if you follow your senses of sight, touch and smell.

looking for the cuisson

Sight Look out for the point at which the flesh turns from translucent to opaque. Sometimes there is a slight pinkness to the flesh, depending on the species. With salmon, the cuisson is reached when the flesh turns from a deep pink colour to a lighter hue.

Touch Fish becomes firmer as it cooks: raw flesh bounces when touched and overcooked flesh is hard. Fish that has reached the perfect cuisson should give very slightly when you press it, indicating that it is still moist inside.

Texture Cooked fish generally has a meaty flakiness to it. You should be able to prise a flake or two gently apart.

Smell Perfectly cooked fish smells deliciously appetizing and certainly fuller in its aroma than raw fish.

One other point to bear in mind when judging the cuisson: fish carries on cooking after it has been removed from the pan because of residual heat within it, so always let it stand for a few minutes before serving.

I frequently pan-'roast' fish, first frying it on top of the stove. After browning the fish on both sides, I finish off the cooking in a moderately hot oven, generally for about 5 minutes or so, depending on the thickness of the fish. This makes it easier to control the cooking process. For small quantities, you may not think it is worth turning on the oven and so can just carry on to finish the cooking on top of the stove.

pan-roasting and pan-frying

For the best results, use a heavy-based, high-quality stainless steel pan with a non-stick coating. Heat your pan well over a medium to high heat before adding any oil. Once you are sure that the pan is hot, add a little olive oil and heat well before putting in the fish. The high heat caramelizes the fish proteins and browns the flesh attractively, and this heightens the flavour. (If the fish has been marinating in an oil-based mixture, there is no need to heat any extra oil.) The browning process only takes a matter of minutes, so be sure not to leave the pan once you have added the fish, or it will quickly burn.

Fish served with the skin left on, such as bass, mullet or salmon, is

always cooked skin side down first to give it time to crisp. About 90 per cent of the cooking time is done on this side. The remainder, on the other side, is counted in seconds – just enough to colour the top. For skinned fish, you can divide the time equally between both sides. Then, if you are finishing the cooking in the oven, transfer the pan to the preheated oven. For this you will need a pan with an ovenproof handle.

Best varieties for pan-roasting

Thin fillets from any type of fish, most shellfish (particularly scallops), with the exception of oysters, and squid.

Chef's tip

Season the fish with salt just before you put it in the pan – if you add salt too far ahead, juices will form on the surface and the flesh won't caramelize and brown as well.

When done correctly, grilling and barbecuing are delectable ways of cooking fish, although it is all too easy to burn the surface of the fish before the inside is cooked and juicy. In a busy restaurant kitchen, the risk of getting it wrong is especially high but, for the home cook, where the situation is calmer, grilling and barbecuing are far more feasible cooking methods.

grilling and barbecuing

Griddle pans, also called ridged grill pans, are best for grilling fish. They are easy to buy from good cookware shops or are available by mail order. Choose one with a heavy, solid base that holds heat well. Heat the empty griddle slowly until you can feel a steady heat rising. Using a wad of kitchen paper towels, lightly oil the hot pan. Press a fish fillet or whole gutted fish on to the ridges and cook for about 3 minutes without moving the fish. This helps the fish to take on the characteristic chargrilled stripes and prevents it from sticking.

If you prefer to use a top-heat grill, preheat the grill to hot, then turn the heat down to medium before adding the fish. Lightly oil the bars of the grill rack if you like, wiping them with some kitchen paper towel dipped in oil.

To grill fish on a barbecue, make sure the flames have died right down to an ashy glow and you can barely see any flame; you should feel a nice even heat rising. If using real charcoal (rather than gas or electric heat), allow a good 30–45 minutes for this stage to be reached. Use tongs to turn the fish, and allow it to brown evenly on both sides.

Fillets of monkfish, either whole or cut into portions, make a marvellous outdoor roast, especially when they have been spiked with rosemary or thyme. If you wish, add a few herbs or aromatic twigs to the ashes to impart extra flavour. Marinate the fish first in an oily dressing and baste frequently during cooking. You might also like to drizzle the fish with wine, a light beer or water during cooking, just to keep it moist.

Best varieties for grilling and barbecuing

Firm or oily fish, such as salmon, trout, mackerel and sturgeon, with the skin left on. Barbecuing is especially suitable for prawns and langoustines in their shells, gutted fresh sardines (use one of those fish racks shaped like a wheel to grill several at once) and cubes of monkfish or tuna, which can be threaded on to wooden satay sticks. Soak these in cold water for half an hour beforehand so the wood doesn't burn too much.

Chef's tip

The bars of a grill will determine what the cooked fish will look like, so make sure they will leave an attractive pattern, and that they are sufficiently close together to hold small fish or shellfish. When barbecuing, you'll also find a special fish rack useful because turning grilled fish can be a delicate operation if the flesh is not to be broken.

My favourite way of cooking fish is poaching it in a court-bouillon (page 58). I really feel this method does true justice to the natural flavours and tender texture of fish. It is also a very convenient way of cooking and serving it, because you can poach the garnish with the fish at the same time and serve both without losing heat, or running the risk of the fish overcooking. It is the ultimate all-in-one method.

poaching

Half-fill a shallow pan with court-bouillon and bring to the boil. Turn the heat right down to a gentle simmer – only the occasional bubble should break on the surface. Slide the prepared fish fillets or tranches into the liquor. Cook for about 5 minutes, or until the flesh feels just firm. When poached, simply cover the cooked fish with a butter wrapper and keep warm in an oven on low until you are ready to serve. Don't leave it for too long, however, or the fish will overcook.

Best varieties for poaching

Monkfish, halibut, turbot, cod and salmon can all be served with their poaching liquor. Simply remove the fish from the pan and boil the liquor until reduced by half. Add some tarragon sprigs to infuse in the liquor and finish with a little coarse-grained mustard, double cream and chopped fresh dill.

Lobster can be gently poached, then left to cool in the cooking liquor (this completes the cooking process very gently). Scallops, oysters, mussels, cuttlefish and clams can be cooked in or out of their shells. Use the cooking liquor as the base of a light soup.

Chef's tip

You can vary the poaching liquor depending on the fish and the recipe. For example, monkfish, skate and John Dory are all wonderful poached in a court-bouillon that is flavoured and coloured with saffron. The court-bouillon can then be reduced down in a wide, shallow pan and used as the base of an accompanying sauce. Turbot is excellent cooked in a red wine court-bouillon. The wine stains the skin, making a sharp contrast in colour with the creamy flesh inside.

This method can involve both cooking on the hob and then, with liquid, in the oven, or just the cooking in the oven, depending on the thickness of the fish. Frequent basting as the stock reduces down gives the top of the fish a glossy, inviting glaze. You will need to use a heavy-based metal frying pan that has a heat-resistant handle. Cast-iron pans are ideal for braising.

braising

1 To braise by combining stovetop and oven cooking: following the instructions for pan-roasting (page 45), quickly caramelize the outside of the fish in a hot pan on top of the stove.

2 When the fish has browned, pour in enough fish stock to come just halfway up the fish.

3 Dot with butter and transfer to a medium hot oven, uncovered, to braise. Leave to cook for a few minutes, basting once or twice by spooning the pan juices over the fish. (There is no need to turn the fish.) The basting process is crucial to prevent the top of the fish from becoming dry, but it does mean you can't leave it unattended.

Best varieties for braising

Thick fillets of John Dory, turbot, cod, brill and monkfish, as well as most whole fish, especially large Dover soles, John Dory, snappers and smaller sea bass.

Chef's tip

To make a quick sauce, remove the fish from the pan. Stir a little white wine into the pan juices and allow to reduce, then stir in a knob of butter and a splash of cream. Season, then pour over the fish.

Small pieces of fish and shellfish are perfect for this traditional and delicious method of cooking. Dip the seafood in batter (see beignets of oysters on page 107) or coat in beaten egg and crumbs (unsweetened brioche crumbs, fine dried white breadcrumbs or grissini breadstick crumbs), then lower gently into hot oil and fry to a beautifully crisp, golden-brown morsel.

deep-frying

Use light oils for deep-frying such as groundnut (arachide or peanut) or sunflower oil. Although vegetable-oil blends and corn oil are good for frying at high temperatures, they are quite heavy in flavour, making them suitable for chips but not for fish. Pure olive oil (not extra-virgin) is fine for deep-frying in small quantities, but the oil burns at very high temperatures, which makes it unsuitable for frying in large quantities.

Fish should be cut into pieces of an even thickness, but not too thick or the outside could become dry before the inside is tender. A thickness of 3cm is about the maximum. Dip first in seasoned flour and shake off the excess. Then dunk in a shallow bowl of beaten egg to coat thoroughly, and drain well. Finally, drop into a shallow bowl of fine dried breadcrumbs, and shake off the excess. You can repeat the process a second time for a thicker coat. I prefer just one light, crisp coat.

It is important that the oil is very hot, about 180–190°C/350–375°F, and the coated pieces of fish should be lowered carefully into it to seal the coating. If the fish is quite thick or needs longer cooking, then cook the outside first for a minute or so, lift out of the oil with a draining spoon or basket, lower the heat of the oil to 160°C/325°F and cook for a further 3–5 minutes. In general, fish pieces are best cooked at around 180°C/350°F for approximately 2–3 minutes. Reheat the oil in between batches. A deep-frying thermometer is useful, or, better still, a deep-fat fryer with thermostatic control.

Safety hint
Never leave a heated deep-fat fryer unattended, even to answer the phone or front door bell, unless the model you are using has a built-in thermostat.

Best varieties for deep-frying

Thin fillets of white fish, rings of squid, scallops (sliced in half first), shelled langoustines or large prawns, miniature mackerels and sardines. Avoid using richer fish, such as salmon or monkfish.

Herb leaves are also good deep-fried and make an eye-catching garnish; parsley, basil, chervil or sage are all suitable. Use large, flat leaves and make sure they are completely dry. Lower them into the hot oil using a frying basket and fry for a minute or so, then drain on kitchen paper towels.

Chef's tip

To prevent crumby egg or soggy crumbs, coat all the fish pieces at the same time at each stage – toss all in flour at once, then dip all in egg, wipe your fingers and coat all in crumbs.

This is a quick process which gives a light and moist result. The purpose of steaming is to keep the flesh of the fish delicate but, as it can break up easily, great care is needed. In fact, steaming can be trickier than pan-roasting as the fish is cooked quite quickly and so demands close attention. However, with steaming, the cuisson is easier to judge than with other cooking methods.

steaming

I use a large stainless steel steamer in my kitchen, but for home use I suggest that you invest in a tower of Chinese bamboo baskets. These are highly affordable and available from Oriental food markets and some kitchen shops. In addition to steaming, you can use them for reheating a complete meal or a number of dishes at a time. Pay attention to the water underneath. For simple steaming, you can add crushed parsley stalks, whole spices, bay leaves, sliced onions, carrot and fennel. You could add wine to the liquid too, or lemon juice and strips of zest. Use whatever you feel is appropriate to the fish cooking gently above the liquid.

Bring a pan of water or light stock to the boil. Place the fish or shellfish on a heatproof dish, or, as here, on a bed of fresh seaweed, in the steamer. Season lightly. Cover the steamer and place over the pan. Steam for 5–10 minutes, depending on the thickness of the fish.

Best varieties for steaming

Most fish, especially chunky cod, fillets of whiting and other white fish; my current favourite is baby mackerel, which the French call oisette. You can wrap the fish first in other foods to give colour as well as flavour. Try cod in spinach or chard leaves, or John Dory fillets in skinned and roasted pepper shells. To retain moisture, it helps to place fish for steaming on a butter wrapper or seasoned foil (or seaweed). Shellfish for steaming include scallops, loosened and cleaned first, then left in their shells; coquillage (a glorious collection of shellfish such as clams, cockles and winkles); and oysters, which open up in the steam. Take care when removing the steamed fish that you don't spill any of the delicious juices.

Chef's tip

Season fish twice: just before steaming, as normal, and again after cooking.

A working restaurant kitchen rarely needs to use a microwave, as there are steamers or frying pans constantly on the go for cooking fish quickly. In the home, however, a microwave is convenient for cooking fish, and produces a similar texture to poaching or steaming. A microwave works by heating and cooking food from within, but it cannot brown the food on its own – for this you need a special browning plate.

microwaving

Microwave ovens are ideal for fish, as the fish simply cooks in its own juices. Make sure the piece is an even size and place the thickest part of the fish or fish pieces in the centre of the dish. The dish should be non-metallic and heatproof. Season the fish or flavour it lightly, then brush with a small amount of olive oil, or cover with cling film, a non-metallic butter wrapper or crumpled wet greaseproof paper, and cook for the recommended time. It is not possible to give exact times as each microwave differs in power output, from 500 to 1000 watts or more.

Best varieties for microwaving

All fish can be microwaved, but some varieties of shellfish, such as scallops, cook so quickly on the hob that it's not worth using the microwave.

Chef's tip

Microwaves are also useful for cooking fish stocks. Chop up the bones, vegetables and other ingredients, place in a large heatproof glass bowl and cover with cold water. Cover with a piece of cling film folded back very slightly at one edge to allow a whisper of steam to escape during cooking. Switch the microwave on to full (or 100 per cent) power and heat for 15–20 minutes. The microwave will turn itself off so there is no risk of the stock boiling dry. Strain the stock and return it to the microwave, uncovered. Cook for an additional 10 minutes or so to reduce down.

2

recipes

stocks, sauces and dressings

stocks

court-bouillon

This light vegetable stock with wine and lemon is useful for poaching fish, giving it a moist texture and full flavour. The court-bouillon can be reused up to three times, but don't be tempted to use leftover court-bouillon as a stock for soups and sauces as it is too acidic. You can make batches of court-bouillon to freeze and use at a later date. Freeze the concentrated stock in two 500ml blocks. When frozen, remove from the moulds and store each block in a separate freezer bag. Remember to label and date them. Unsalted stock should keep for up to 1 month.

Makes about 2 litres

4 leeks, roughly chopped
4 carrots, roughly chopped
2 celery sticks, roughly chopped
3 onions, roughly chopped
3 medium shallots, roughly chopped
1 bulb fennel, chopped
6 cloves garlic, unpeeled
1 large sprig each fresh thyme, tarragon, basil and parsley, tied together
¼ tsp white peppercorns
25g rock salt
2 lemons, sliced
4 star anise
400ml dry white wine

1   Place the leeks, carrots, celery, onions, shallots, fennel, garlic and herbs in a stockpot or saucepan. Cover with 2.5 litres of cold water and bring to the boil.
2   Add the peppercorns, salt, lemon slices and star anise. Pour in the white wine and bring to the boil again, then simmer gently for about 30 minutes.
3   Line a colander with a large piece of wet muslin and set it over a deep bowl or jug. Strain the court-bouillon through the colander and discard the vegetables, herbs, spices and lemon. Store in the fridge, covered, and use within 3 days, or freeze in 500ml or 1 litre blocks and use within 1 month.

fish stock

A good fish stock depends on the quality of the fishbones used to make it, so ask your fishmonger to save you the best ones. Turbot and sole bones have a good flavour and are suitably light in colour, whereas the bones of some fish, such as mackerel and herring, tend to be too oily. Bones from a medium turbot should be sufficient. Haddock or hake bones will also do, or you can use a mixture. You can use the head of a large fish, but remember to cut out the eyes and the gills, wash out any traces of blood and chop the head in half. Avoid using any fish skin, as far as possible. No salt is added to the stocks – that comes later, when they are used in the recipes. There are a number of ways to vary the flavour of a basic fish stock. One of the simplest is to add about 250g of smoked bacon pieces, including the rinds and bone. Bacon gives a tangy, slightly smoky flavour.

Makes about 1.5 litres

1 medium leek, chopped
1 medium onion, chopped
1 celery stick, chopped
½ bulb fennel, chopped
2 cloves garlic, unpeeled
100ml olive oil (not extra-virgin)
about 1.5kg white fish bones and head, cleaned and roughly chopped
300ml dry white wine
2 sprigs each fresh thyme and parsley, tied together
½ lemon, sliced
¼ tsp white peppercorns

1   Put the leek, onion, celery, fennel and garlic into a stockpot or large saucepan. Add the oil and heat until the vegetables start to sizzle. Gently sweat the vegetables on a low heat, covered, for about 15 minutes, until softened.
2   Stir in the fishbones and head, and the wine and cook until almost all the

ingredients for salmon and orange stock

liquid has evaporated. Pour in 2 litres of cold water and add the herbs, lemon and peppercorns. Bring to the boil, skimming off the scum off the surface with a wide spoon.

3   Reduce the heat and simmer, uncovered, for 20 minutes, no longer. Remove from the heat and leave to settle for about 10 minutes.

4   Line a large colander with wet muslin and set over a large bowl. Carefully strain the liquid through the muslin, removing the larger bones with a draining spoon first. If you are not using it straight away, cool, then chill and use within 3 days, or freeze in 500ml or 1 litre blocks and use within 1 month. For a more concentrated flavour, you can boil the stock down to about 1 litre.

salmon and orange stock

Follow the recipe for Fish Stock (opposite), but use only salmon bones, including a cleaned and split head, and substitute freshly squeezed orange juice for the wine. Before making the stock, roast the salmon bones in an oven preheated to 200°C/400°F/Gas Mark 6 for 15–20 minutes. This gives a good flavour and has the added bonus of preventing scum forming during boiling.

vegetable nage

This is one of my favourite stocks because it is so light. The vegetables are left to float in the liquid for 24 hours before straining, thus infusing the nage with their subtle flavours.

Makes about 1.5 litres

3 onions, roughly chopped
1 leek, roughly chopped
2 celery sticks, roughly chopped
6 carrots, roughly chopped
1 head garlic, split in half
1 lemon, roughly chopped
¼ tsp white peppercorns
¼ tsp pink peppercorns
1 small bay leaf
4 star anise
1 sprig each fresh tarragon, basil, coriander, thyme, parsley and chervil, tied together
200ml dry white wine

1   Put the onions, leek, celery and carrots into a stockpot or large saucepan. Add the garlic, lemon, peppercorns, bay leaf and star anise. Pour in 2 litres of cold water. Bring to the boil, then simmer for 10 minutes.

2   Remove from the heat and push the herbs into the liquid. Pour in the wine and stir. Set aside to cool.

3   When cool, transfer the stock to a large jug or bowl. Cover and chill for about 24 hours.

4   The next day, strain through a muslin-lined colander into a jug or bowl. Discard the vegetables, herbs and spices. Keep in the fridge and use within 3 days, or freeze in 500ml or 1 litre blocks and use within 1 month.

chicken stock

It may surprise you to find a meat stock in a seafood cookery book, but light meats and fish do go well together. Chicken with prawns, and bacon with smoked fish, are two good combinations that come to mind. For this reason, I often use a chicken stock with fish soups and sauces.

Makes about 2 litres

2kg raw chicken carcasses, roughly chopped, or bony chicken wings or backs
3 celery sticks, roughly chopped
2 leeks, roughly chopped
2 onions, roughly chopped
2 large carrots, roughly chopped
½ head garlic, unpeeled
1 large sprig fresh thyme
20g rock salt

1   Put the chicken carcasses in a stockpot or large saucepan. Cover with 4 litres of cold water and bring to the boil, skimming off any scum from the surface with a slotted spoon.

2   Add the celery, leeks, onions and carrots to the pan, together with the garlic, thyme and salt. Return to the boil, then simmer, uncovered, for about 3 hours, skimming when necessary.

3   Line a colander with muslin, then strain the stock through it into a large bowl. Discard the bones, vegetables and herbs. (For a stronger stock, return the liquid to the pan and boil until reduced by half.)

4   Cool, chill and use within 3 days, or freeze in 500ml or 1 litre blocks and use within 1 month.

brown chicken stock

Some recipes require a dark chicken stock. For this, first roast the chicken bones in an oven preheated to 200°C/400°F/Gas Mark 6 for 15–20 minutes, turning them once or twice, until dark golden brown, then proceed with the recipe above.

vegetable nage

sauces

fish velouté with cream

A good all-purpose sauce, this can be used as the basis for a richer sauce, or served in its own right as a classic fish sauce. It turns the simplest of meals, such as a grilled fillet of fish and baby Jersey Royal new potatoes, into a treat.

Makes about 500ml

15g butter

4 shallots, finely chopped

250ml dry white wine

250ml Noilly Prat or other dry vermouth

500ml Fish Stock (pages 58–59)

250ml double cream

250ml single cream

sea salt and freshly ground black pepper

1   Heat the butter in a wide saucepan. Stir in the shallots and gently fry for about 15 minutes until softened, but not coloured. Add the wine and vermouth, bring to the boil and boil for about 7 minutes, or until reduced by half.

2   Pour in the stock and bring back to the boil, stirring. Continue to boil until reduced by half. Stir in both creams and return to a gentle boil. Simmer until the sauce is the consistency of pouring cream. Season with salt and pepper.

3   Strain the sauce through a fine sieve into a jug or bowl. The sauce should be smooth and glossy. Use straight away,

or chill for up to 2 days. You can freeze the sauce in single portions for 1 month. Thaw gently from frozen in a saucepan or in a microwave oven on low power.

fish velouté without cream

Like all good chefs, I pride myself on making memorable sauces that are thickened in the time-honoured way of boiling down to reduce the liquid. But I do find certain occasions call for a less rich velouté, one with far less (or no) cream. You should find this version useful for simple supper dishes or to serve with fish meals to children.

Makes about 750ml

500ml Fish Stock (pages 58–59)

250ml milk

50g butter

2 level tbsp flour

1 tbsp double cream (optional)

sea salt and freshly ground black pepper

1   Pour the stock and milk into a saucepan. Bring to the boil, taking care not to boil over. Remove from the heat and pour into a jug.

2   In a heavy-based saucepan, heat the butter to just sizzling. Stir in the flour, then cook on a very gentle heat until the mixture becomes a blond-coloured paste, about 3–5 minutes.

3   Pour in the milky stock, a little at a time, mixing it into the paste with a wooden spoon. Take care to blend each amount of stock until smooth and creamy before adding the next, to prevent lumps from forming.

4   When all the liquid has been added, simmer for a minute or two. Stir in the cream, if using, then season and serve. (If you are making the sauce ahead of time, cover the top with crumpled wet greaseproof paper to stop a skin from forming, and keep warm.)

parsley sauce

To make parsley sauce, blanch about 6 tablespoons chopped fresh parsley, purée, then add to the velouté just before serving. This sauce goes particularly well with smoked haddock and creamy mash.

sauce thermidor

A variation of a velouté sauce without cream, this goes famously well with lobster, although it is also equally good with pan-fried scallops. Thermidor was the name of the eleventh month in the French Revolutionary calendar. Why that episode is associated with luxury lobster escapes my knowledge, but at least you know half the story.

Makes about 300ml

Fish Velouté without Cream (opposite)
made with 100ml Fish Stock
(pages 58–59) 100ml milk, 20g butter
and 2 tsp flour
50g butter
50g finely chopped shallots
100ml dry white wine
200ml Fish Stock (pages 58-59)
100ml double cream
2 tsp Dijon mustard
sea salt and freshly ground black pepper
2 small knobs of ice-cold butter to finish

1 Make up the fish velouté without
cream. Set aside.

2 In a heavy-based medium
saucepan, melt the butter. Gently sweat
the shallots, covered, for 10 minutes or
until softened, but not coloured. Pour
in the wine and bring to the boil. Cook,
uncovered, until almost all of the liquid
has evaporated.

3 Pour in the fish stock and boil until
reduced by two-thirds. Stir in the fish
velouté and return to the boil. Simmer
for 5 minutes.

4 Mix in the cream and bring back to
the boil. Stir in the mustard and season
if necessary.

5 Just before serving, whisk in the
knobs of ice-cold butter to give the
sauce a glossy sheen.

simple sauternes sauce

This is a really easy sauce to make,
especially if you've got a little leftover
fish stock, or a small frozen block in the
freezer. Fish and sweet white wine
partner each other well, and this simple
sauce is excellent with sole or turbot.
Keep a packet of butter in the freezer for
use here and in other sauces which call
for ice-cold butter.

Makes about 300ml

150ml Sauternes or other dessert wine
150ml Fish Stock (pages 58–59)
50g ice-cold unsalted butter, diced
sea salt and freshly ground
white pepper

1 Boil the wine in a small saucepan
until reduced by half (to approximately
4 tablespoons). Add the stock and boil
again until reduced by half.

2 Using a small balloon whisk,
gradually beat in the chilled, diced butter
until the sauce is smooth and glossy.
Season and remove from the heat.
Allow to cool for a few minutes, stirring
once or twice, then serve.

claret sauce

This recipe must come as a complete
surprise to the plain-cooking brigade – a
fish sauce made with chicken stock, fish
stock and red wine. Trust me, it works a
treat with salmon, mullet and chargrilled
tuna, as well as with other meaty,
full-flavoured fish.

Makes about 400ml

350ml claret or other red wine
200ml Brown Chicken Stock (page 61)
300ml Fish Stock (pages 58–59)
2 medium shallots, finely chopped
50g button mushrooms, finely chopped
1 fresh bouquet garni (page 39)
100ml double cream
200g ice-cold butter, diced
sea salt and freshly ground black pepper

1 Pour the wine, brown chicken stock
and fish stock into a large saucepan.
Add the shallots, mushrooms and
bouquet garni and bring to the boil.
Simmer, uncovered, until the liquid is
reduced by about two-thirds.

2 Remove the bouquet garni, then stir
in the cream. Bring back to the boil for a
few seconds.

3 Strain the liquid through a sieve set
over a bowl. Pour the strained liquid
back into the saucepan and simmer
gently for about 5 minutes.

4 Using a small balloon whisk,
gradually beat in the chilled, diced butter
until the sauce is smooth and glossy.
Season and serve hot. If making the

sauce in advance, cover the top with a butter wrapper, cling film or crumpled wet greaseproof paper to stop a skin from forming, and keep warm.

classic champagne butter sauce

Butter is used to thicken and enrich this sauce, yet it tastes light and delicate. Use Dutch or Normandy unsalted butter for the best flavour. For a red butter sauce, substitute red wine vinegar and fine red wine for the Champagne vinegar and Champagne.

Makes 500ml

1 medium shallot, finely chopped
4 tbsp Champagne vinegar
1 sprig each fresh thyme and tarragon
200ml Champagne or other good dry
  sparkling white wine
250g ice-cold butter, diced
1 tbsp double cream
sea salt and freshly ground
  white pepper

1　Put the shallot, vinegar, thyme and tarragon in a saucepan. Cook gently for about 5 minutes, or until the shallots are softened and the vinegar has reduced to a syrup. Pour in the Champagne and cook gently, uncovered, until reduced by half. Remove the herbs.

2　Using a balloon whisk, gradually beat in the chilled, diced butter over a gentle heat. Make sure that each piece of butter is well incorporated before adding the next and that the sauce does not boil, otherwise it will curdle.

3　When all the butter has been incorporated, stir in the cream, then season to taste. For extra smoothness, pass the sauce through a sieve, rubbing with the back of a ladle or a wooden spoon. Serve warm, if necessary stirring occasionally to prevent a skin from forming.

olive oil hollandaise

My version of this classic French fish sauce is made in a Mediterranean style by using olive oil instead of melted butter, or a mixture of the two. Whisking the eggs to a creamy sabayon consistency (page 219) gives a firmer base for the sauce and minimizes the risk of curdling. Use a lighter pure olive oil for this, rather than a heavy extra-virgin oil, or even mix with a half quantity of sunflower or groundnut oil. Reducing vinegar down to obtain such a tiny amount is impractical. Instead, simply boil down the contents of a small bottle of good white wine vinegar until reduced by half, then cool and rebottle.

Makes about 300ml

6 coriander seeds, finely crushed
3 egg yolks
200ml light olive oil, warmed
2 tsp reduced white wine vinegar
  (see recipe introduction)
squeeze of fresh lemon juice
good pinch cayenne pepper
sea salt and freshly ground black pepper

1　Put the crushed coriander seeds, egg yolks and 1 tablespoon of warm water into a heatproof bowl (one that will sit snugly over a saucepan). Pour a little water into the saucepan and heat to a gentle simmer. Sit the bowl on top.

2　Beat the egg-yolk mixture with a balloon whisk or a hand-held electric mixer, until pale gold and creamy and the mixture will leave a firm trail on itself when the whisk is lifted out. Remove the bowl from the heat and continue whisking for about 3 minutes until the mixture is cool. Slowly add the warmed olive oil – start by dipping a tablespoon in the oil and letting the oil slowly trickle in from the tip. Continue to whisk as you gradually incorporate the oil. As the mixture thickens, add more oil in stages, but don't be tempted to add too much at once. (If the mixture looks as if it might start to curdle, don't panic – add a drop or two of cold water and whisk again.)

from front: sauce maltaise, mustard seed and mint hollandaise, olive oil hollandaise

3   When all the oil has been added, beat in the reduced vinegar and the lemon juice. Season with the cayenne, salt and pepper. Serve warm. If making the hollandaise a short while before serving, spoon into a wide-necked vacuum flask to keep warm.

classic hollandaise

Simply substitute 200ml clarified butter (page 218) for the olive oil.

mustard seed and mint hollandaise

This version of hollandaise is flavoured with a lively combination of hot mustard and cool mint, making it an unusual accompaniment for grilled fish.

Makes about 300ml

300ml Olive Oil Hollandaise (page 64)
2 tsp coarse-grained mustard
1 tsp finely chopped fresh mint
sea salt and freshly ground black pepper

1   Make up the hollandaise sauce.
2   Stir the mustard and chopped mint into the sauce. You may wish to thin the sauce slightly by adding a little warm water. Season and serve straight away.

sauce mousseline

This is a frothier, creamier hollandaise sauce; it is especially good with delicate soles or sea bass.

Makes about 300ml

300ml Classic Hollandaise (left)
100ml whipping cream
squeeze of fresh lemon juice
sea salt and freshly ground black pepper

1   Make up the classic hollandaise sauce and keep warm.
2   Whip the cream until it holds soft peaks. Fold gently into the warm sauce. Stir in the lemon juice and season to taste. Serve straight away.

sauce maltaise

Orange is a good flavour with richer fish such as salmon or even lobster.

Makes about 300ml

300ml Olive Oil Hollandaise (page 64)
grated zest of 1 blood orange
100ml fresh blood orange juice
sea salt and freshly ground black pepper

1   Make up the hollandaise sauce and keep warm.
2   Put the orange zest and juice into a saucepan. Boil until reduced to about 3 tablespoons. Whisk into the sauce. Check the seasoning and serve.

mustard mayonnaise

Like a hollandaise sauce, a mayonnaise is what we call an emulsion sauce of oil and 'water' (eggs) held in suspension with grainy seasonings. Use a balloon whisk to combine all the ingredients, and take care to drip in the oil slowly at first, so that the mayonnaise holds together.

Makes about 300ml

2 egg yolks
1 tsp white wine vinegar
1 tsp English mustard powder
300ml groundnut oil
sea salt and freshly ground black pepper

1   Put the egg yolks, vinegar and mustard in a bowl. Season well and stand the bowl on a damp cloth. Whisk well until smooth and creamy.
2   Dip a teaspoon into the oil and trickle a drip or two from the tip of the spoon into the yolks. Whisk the mixture hard as you add the oil.
3   Repeat several times, adding the oil drip by drip. Then gradually increase the amount of oil, making sure each new addition is well incorporated before adding the next. This ensures that you produce a thick mayonnaise. If your mayonnaise curdles, simply whisk another egg yolk with a pinch each of salt, pepper and mustard in a separate bowl. Whisk the curdled mixture into the extra yolk mixture and it should emulsify.
4   Once all the oil has been added, mix in a tablespoon or two of cold water to stabilize the emulsion. Check the seasoning and serve. The mayonnaise should keep well in a sealed container in the fridge for up to 1 week.

aïoli

There are no half measures with a good aïoli. It is a very garlicky sauce, if made traditionally. Add less garlic if you're not much of a fan but, be warned, it will still have a strong smell.

Makes about 300ml

300ml Mustard Mayonnaise (opposite)
10 cloves fresh garlic
1 tsp sea salt
pinch saffron strands
freshly ground black pepper

1   Make up the mustard mayonnaise.
2   Peel the garlic by laying each clove in turn on a board and placing a large heavy-bladed knife flat on top. Smash your fist down on top to crush the clove and you'll find the skin slips off easily.
3   Roughly chop the cloves, then sprinkle with the salt. Crush all the garlic to a fine pulp using the tip of the knife.
4   Beat this into the mayonnaise, crushing in the saffron stands as you mix. Season with pepper and serve.

tartare sauce

This sauce is always good with crispy, deep-fried fish, and this is my favourite recipe because it is quite a delicate version of the original. If you prefer a strong tartare sauce flavour, then simply double the quantity of finely chopped flavouring ingredients.

Makes 300ml

300ml Mustard Mayonnaise (opposite)
1 tsp finely chopped gherkins
1 tsp finely chopped capers
1 tsp finely chopped pitted
   green olives
1 tsp finely chopped pitted
   black olives
1 tsp finely chopped fresh parsley
sea salt and freshly ground black pepper

1   Make up the mustard mayonnaise.
2   Stir in all of the finely chopped flavouring ingredients. Check the seasoning and serve straight away.

rémoulade sauce

Rémoulade is good with salmon or mackerel, and also sensational with fish cakes – my favourite.

Makes about 300ml

300ml Mustard Mayonnaise (opposite)
25g gherkins, finely chopped
25g capers, finely chopped
1 anchovy fillet, finely chopped
1 tsp Dijon mustard
1 tsp finely chopped fresh chervil
1 tsp finely chopped fresh parsley
1 tsp finely chopped fresh tarragon
sea salt and freshly ground pepper

1   Make up the mustard mayonnaise.
2   Mix all the remaining ingredients into the sauce, stirring thoroughly. Check the seasoning and serve.

red pepper sabayon

This is an attractive pinky-red butter sauce to serve at barbecues and picnics, and is especially good with Mediterranean or tropical fish.

Makes about 400ml

2 large red peppers, finely chopped
70g chilled butter, diced
1 sprig each fresh thyme and tarragon
200ml Vegetable Nage (page 61)
3 egg yolks
sea salt and freshly ground black pepper

1   Heat the peppers and a quarter of the butter in a saucepan until sizzling. Stir in the thyme and tarragon. Cook gently, stirring once or twice, for a minute, then add the vegetable nage and continue cooking over a low heat for about 10 minutes, uncovered, until the peppers are softened.
2   Remove the herbs and pour the mixture into a food processor. Blend until smooth and creamy, then pass through a sieve, rubbing with the back of a ladle or a wooden spoon. Allow to cool to room temperature. Meanwhile, chill a mixing bowl.
3   Pour the red pepper purée into the cold mixing bowl, then beat in the egg yolks (chilling the bowl prevents the yolks from curdling). Place the bowl over a pan of gently simmering water, making sure the bowl is not in contact with the

water. Using a balloon whisk or a hand-held electric mixer, beat until thick and creamy and the mixture leaves a trail on itself when the whisk is lifted out.

4   Gradually whisk in the remaining chilled, diced butter until the sauce is smooth and creamy. Check the seasoning and serve straight away.

mango sauce

This fruity relish is particularly delicious with barbecued fish, grilled salmon or cooked lobster or langoustines. Make batches of it, especially during the summer months, to serve outdoors for picnics and barbecues.

Makes about 500ml

2 small ripe mangoes, finely chopped
3 tbsp Cognac or other brandy
1 tbsp green peppercorns in brine, drained
good pinch curry powder
300ml Fish Stock (pages 58–59)
200ml double cream
100g natural yogurt or crème fraîche
1 tsp chopped fresh parsley
sea salt and freshly ground black pepper

1   Put the mangoes, brandy, peppercorns and curry powder in a saucepan. Cook gently for about 3 minutes, or until lightly softened. Pour in the fish stock and bring to the boil.

Simmer for about 20 minutes, stirring occasionally. Add the cream, then return to a gentle boil, stirring, and simmer for 3 minutes. Remove from the heat.

2   Pour the mixture into a food processor. Add the yogurt or crème fraîche and process until smooth and creamy, scraping down the sides of the container once or twice.

3   Pass the mixture through a sieve into the saucepan, rubbing with the back of a ladle or a wooden spoon. Check the seasoning, then stir in the parsley. Reheat gently, but do not allow to boil, then serve. Alternatively, allow to cool and transfer to a screw-top jar to serve cold. Store in the fridge for up to 1 week; the sauce cannot be frozen.

sauce américaine

This is the ultimate lobster sauce, which never fails to lift even the simplest grilled or poached fish to ethereal heights. You can serve it with chicken or grilled seafood as well. This is a good recipe to make after a lobster feast because the sauce requires the shells and heads.

Makes about 500ml

shells and heads of 2 medium lobsters
1 tbsp olive oil
1 medium onion, finely chopped
2 carrots, finely chopped
1 large clove garlic, crushed

2 tsp Cognac or other brandy
200ml Noilly Prat or other dry vermouth
1 tbsp flour
300ml Fish Stock (pages 58–59)
3 plum tomatoes, skinned, de-seeded and chopped
1 large fresh bouquet garni (page 39)
100ml double cream
good pinch cayenne pepper
sea salt and freshly ground black pepper

1   Split the lobster heads in half and remove the soft insides, saving the green corals if you find them. Wash the heads and shells well, and chop up the shells if they are large.

2   Heat the oil in a large saucepan. Sauté the shells for about 5 minutes. Add the onion, carrots and garlic and sauté gently for another 5 minutes, stirring occasionally. Stir in the brandy and cook for a minute until it has evaporated. Pour in the vermouth and simmer until reduced by half.

3   Sprinkle in the flour and mix well. Pour in the stock and bring to the boil. Stir in the chopped tomatoes and bouquet garni. Whisk in the lobster corals too, if you have them. Return to the boil, stirring. Simmer, uncovered, for 15–20 minutes, or until reduced by half. Remove from the heat.

4   Strain through a sieve and return to the saucepan, discarding the shells, vegetables and bouquet garni. Pour in

the cream and bring back to the boil. Simmer for about 5 minutes until reduced a little. Season with the cayenne, salt and pepper, and serve.

sauce gazpacho

This simple yet pungent tomato sauce brings a rich piquancy to grilled fish and seafood salads.

Makes about 300ml

500g ripe cherry tomatoes

2 tbsp double cream

50g butter, diced

2 tbsp olive oil

sea salt and freshly ground
  black pepper

1   Put the tomatoes in a food processor or blender and process to a smooth purée. Rub through a sieve set over a saucepan.

2   Gently boil the tomato purée until reduced by half. Stir in the cream, diced butter and olive oil.

3   Pour the sauce back into the food processor or blender, and purée the sauce again, then rub through the sieve a second time. Season to taste and serve at room temperature.

sauce vierge

This refreshing coriander and basil dressing is excellent served with juicy, meaty fish such as pan-roasted red mullet and tuna fillets, and also makes an aromatic dipping sauce for plump fresh scallops.

Makes about 150ml

50ml extra-virgin olive oil

1 small shallot, finely chopped

2 tbsp fresh lemon juice

6 coriander seeds

1 ripe tomato, skinned, de-seeded
  and finely diced (optional)

6 large fresh basil leaves, finely
  shredded

6 large fresh coriander leaves,
  finely shredded

½ tsp balsamic vinegar

sea salt and freshly ground
  black pepper

1   In a small saucepan, heat 2 teaspoons of the oil and gently fry the shallot for 10 minutes, or until softened. Add the remaining oil with the lemon juice and gently reheat.

2   Crush the coriander seeds in a pestle and mortar, then add to the pan together with the tomato if using, the shredded basil and coriander and the balsamic vinegar. Season to taste and stir well. Leave to infuse for at least 5 minutes before serving.

sauce gribiche

I find an increasing number of uses for this sauce. It is particularly good combined with many varieties of grilled fish, such as mullet.

Makes about 300ml

2 hard-boiled eggs, halved

1 small shallot, finely chopped

100g gherkins, well drained and
  finely chopped

100g small capers, well drained

2 tsp sherry vinegar

1 tbsp chopped fresh parsley

200ml extra-virgin olive oil

sea salt and freshly ground black pepper

1   Rub the eggs through a metal sieve into a bowl. Mix in the shallot, gherkins, capers, vinegar and parsley.

2   Gradually beat in the oil, then season to taste. The sauce can be stored in the fridge for about 3 days.

fresh harissa frozen in an ice cube tray

fresh harissa

I add this to rouille (opposite), the spicy sauce traditionally served with fish bouillabaisse. Harissa is also good stirred into hot pasta with crème fraîche, and served with pan-roasted or grilled fish fillets. Use fat red chillies, not small, thin fiery chillies. Freeze any leftover harissa in an ice cube tray – this makes it easy to remove only what you need as you need it.

Makes 300ml

4 fresh red chillies
1 large red pepper
pinch saffron strands
1 tsp coriander seeds, crushed
1 tsp tomato purée
sea salt and freshly ground
  black pepper

1   Split the chillies in half and shake out the seeds. Discard the stalks. Peel the red pepper using a swivel vegetable peeler. Discard the core and seeds, then roughly chop the flesh.

2   Put the chillies, red pepper, saffron, crushed coriander seeds and tomato purée in a food processor or blender. Season to taste, then whizz until smooth, scraping down the sides of the container once or twice.

3   Pour into a small screw-top jar and store in the fridge for up to 3 days, or freeze for up to about 2 months.

rouille

In France, this Mediterranean chilli and garlic sauce is stirred into fish soups to enliven the flavour. It can also be served spread on small, crisp rounds of baby baguette to float on top of fish soups, such as a bouillabaisse. Rouille is made in a similar way to mayonnaise, with the addition of fresh breadcrumbs. You will need some fresh harissa for this recipe.

Makes about 300ml

25g fresh white breadcrumbs
3 tbsp Fish Stock (pages 58–59), warmed
1 large fresh red chilli, de-seeded and
  chopped
2 cloves garlic, chopped
1 egg yolk
1 tsp Fresh Harissa (opposite)
200ml olive oil
sea salt and freshly ground
  black pepper

1   In a bowl, soak the breadcrumbs in the warm stock for 5 minutes.
2   Spoon the soaked breadcrumbs into a food processor and add the chilli, garlic, egg yolk, harissa and some seasoning. Whizz until the mixture is creamy, scraping down the sides of the container as necessary.
3   With the blades still rotating on a very slow speed, gradually trickle in the olive oil. Take your time so that the mixture does not curdle.
4   When the oil is thoroughly mixed in and the sauce is a vibrant pinky-red and the consistency of a thick mayonnaise, check the seasoning. Spoon into a screw-top jar and store in the fridge for up to 1 week.

chilli jam

Call it a jam, pickle or relish – this wonderful sauce goes by several different names because of its varied uses. Make up a batch to keep in the fridge, to add to a variety of fish dishes – my current favourite is to serve it with tempura fish, and who knows what other uses I may find for it? Chilli jam also makes a great present, so increase the amount accordingly and give jars of it away to friends.

Makes about 100ml

6 large, fat red chillies, de-seeded (for a
  milder flavour) and finely chopped
1 small red onion, finely chopped
1 large clove garlic, finely chopped
4 spring onions, finely chopped
3cm cube fresh root ginger, peeled
  and finely chopped
1 tbsp olive oil
1 tsp caster sugar
2 tsp sherry vinegar
2 tsp oyster sauce
sea salt and freshly ground
  black pepper

1   Put the chillies, red onion, garlic, spring onions, ginger, oil and caster sugar into a saucepan. Heat gently until sizzling. Cook on a medium heat for about 10 minutes, stirring occasionally, until the contents start to caramelize.
2   Add the vinegar and stir to de-glaze, then bubble until it has evaporated. Add the oyster sauce and cook for a further 3–4 minutes. Season, then cool and spoon into a screw-top jar. Store in the fridge for up to a week or freeze for up to 6 weeks.

chilli jam

butters and pastes

You don't have to go to all the trouble of making a sauce just to dress up a simple fillet of fish, especially the full-flavoured ones such as salmon, red mullet and tuna. Instead, add flavourings to good-quality unsalted butter (I use Normandy butter) and serve shaped into pats or dainty quenelles. Once blended and smooth, spoon the butter in a long sausage shape on a large piece of cling film, then roll in the film until smooth, wrap tightly and chill. Alternatively spoon into a piping bag with a nozzle and pipe out small shapes on to cling film or baking parchment. Again, chill until firm. You can freeze flavoured butters for up to 1 month.

anchovy butter

Use two 50g cans of anchovies for this pungently flavoured butter.

Serves 8–10

100g anchovy fillets in oil, drained and
   patted dry
200g unsalted butter, softened
freshly ground black pepper

Place the anchovy fillets and soft butter in a food processor. Whizz until smooth, scraping down the sides of the container with a spatula once or twice. Season to taste with pepper.

garlic and herb butter

The amount of garlic you use – anything between 5 and 10 cloves – depends entirely on personal taste.

Serves 8–10

5–10 large cloves garlic, peeled
   and crushed
1 tsp each chopped fresh tarragon,
   flat-leaf parsley and rosemary
200g unsalted butter, softened
sea salt and freshly ground
   black pepper

Mix the crushed garlic with the tarragon, parsley and rosemary. Blend into the butter using a wooden spoon. Alternatively, blend the garlic and herbs in a food processor, then gradually work in the butter. Season to taste.

barbecue butter

This works best when the flavoured butter is not too soft. The butter is good for basting seafood when cooking it outdoors over hot coals on a barbecue, or under a top-heat grill.

Serves 8–10

1 tsp Chilli Jam (page 71) or ready-made
   mild chilli sauce
2 tsp runny honey
1 tbsp lemon juice
25g fresh mint leaves, chopped
200g unsalted butter, softened
sea salt and freshly ground
   black pepper

Mix the chilli jam or mild chilli sauce with the honey, lemon juice and chopped mint. Gradually work in the softened butter with a wooden spoon. Season to taste with salt and pepper.

from left to right: classic parsley butter, roquefort butter, garlic and herb butter

paprika butter

Use only fresh paprika for this butter as stale paprika will impart very little flavour or bright colour.

Serves 8–10

200g unsalted butter, softened + good
  extra knob of butter
1 shallot or small onion, finely chopped
1 heaped tsp paprika
sea salt and freshly ground black pepper
Melt the knob of butter in a small saucepan. Gently fry the shallot or onion for 5 minutes, or until softened but not coloured. Stir in the paprika and cook for just a few seconds. Remove from the heat and cool to room temperature. Beat into the softened butter with seasoning to taste until smooth.

roquefort butter

This rich cheese butter is excellent served with various full-flavoured fish, especially halibut. There's no need to add salt, as the cheese is salty.

Serves 8–10

150g Roquefort, de-rinded and at
  room temperature
150g unsalted butter, softened
freshly ground black pepper
Beat the cheese and butter together until smooth using a wooden spoon. Season with pepper to taste.

classic parsley butter

A mixture of both flat-leaf and fresh curly-leaf parsley gives a better flavour than just using a single variety. This butter goes well with delicate flat fish such as sole, and it is also good with sea bass and cod.

Serves 8–10

75g each fresh flat-leaf and curly-leaf
  parsley, finely chopped
200g unsalted butter, softened
sea salt and freshly ground
  black pepper
Beat the finely chopped parsleys into the soft butter using a wooden spoon. Season to taste with salt and pepper.

sea urchin butter

If you can get hold of sea urchins, they make a wonderful flavoured butter that is delicious stirred gently into scrambled eggs, added to a velouté sauce, or tossed into freshly cooked pasta.

Serves 8–10

3–4 large sea urchins, prepared
  (page 37)
200g unsalted butter, softened
Carefully scrape any debris from the sea urchin tongues, then rub them through a fine sieve with the back of a wooden spoon. Beat the resulting purée into the soft butter.

chilli spice mix

I use this spicy mixture as a flavouring paste, in the same way that an Indian cook might use a curry paste, to enhance sauces, dressings or couscous, for example. This recipe makes enough spice mix to fill a standard jam jar. Store it all in the fridge, or give half of it away as a tasty present to a keen fellow cook.

Makes about 300ml

2 red peppers, roughly chopped
1 yellow pepper, roughly chopped
6 large cloves garlic, roughly chopped
50g piece fresh root ginger, peeled and
  roughly chopped
2 mild fresh red chillies, de-seeded
1 tsp cumin seeds
¼ tsp coriander seeds
3 whole star anise, broken
1 tsp mild curry powder
2 good pinches ground mace
2 tbsp sunflower oil + extra to cover
1   Put the peppers, garlic, ginger and chillies in a food processor. Whizz to a really smooth paste, scraping down the sides of the container once or twice.
2   Put the cumin seeds, coriander seeds and star anise pieces into an electric spice mill or a pestle and mortar. Grind to as smooth a powder as possible. Mix with the curry powder and mace.

3   Heat the 2 tablespoons of oil in a frying pan and stir-fry the pepper paste for a minute. Mix in the ground spices and cook over a gentle heat for 3 minutes, stirring once or twice.

4   Spoon into a screw-top jar and cover the surface with a thin layer of sunflower oil. Leave to cool, then seal and store in the fridge for up to 10 days.

tapenade

This aromatic caper and olive paste originally hails from Provence, where it is spread on bread or toast and served as an appetizer. I use my recipe as an all-purpose flavouring: for example, spread on grilled fillets of fish, such as mullet, or as a dip for croûtes.

Makes about 200ml

50g can anchovy fillets in oil,
  well drained
200g pitted black olives
2 tbsp capers, drained
1 clove garlic, crushed
1 tbsp extra-virgin olive oil
olive oil to cover

Simply whizz all the ingredients together in a food processor until smooth. Spoon into a screw-top jar, cover the surface with a thin layer of olive oil and close tightly. The tapenade will keep in the fridge for about 1 week.

fresh pesto

I often use fresh pesto to garnish pan-roasted fish, sometimes thinning it down with water or vinaigrette and spooning it into a squirty bottle to squeeze off pesto squirls. Do make sure the pine kernels are absolutely fresh, as rancid nuts will spoil the pesto and waste a lot of good olive oil and basil. Purists would use a pestle and mortar, but I suggest you use a food processor as this version has a thin sauce consistency.

Makes about 300ml

50g pine kernels
50g garlic cloves, roughly chopped
50g Parmesan cheese, freshly grated
  very finely
30g fresh basil leaves
120ml extra-virgin olive oil

1   Put the pine kernels, garlic and Parmesan in a food processor and whizz to a fine crumbly mixture.

2   With the motor still running, feed the basil leaves into the machine through the funnel. Slowly trickle in the oil and blend until smooth and creamy. Spoon into a screw-top jar and store in the fridge for up to 10 days.

fresh basil purée

This adds superb colour and flavour to sauces for fish – a very simple idea is given in the recipe for tuna on page 136. You can also use it to colour pasta dough (page 132 – add 2 teaspoons in place of one of the eggs).

Makes about 30ml

1 large bunch fresh basil

1   Pick the leaves from the bunch of basil. Blanch them in boiling water for just a minute, then drain and rinse under cold running water. Drain well again and dry on kitchen paper towel.

2   Blend in a food processor or blender to a very fine purée, scraping down the sides of the container once or twice. Rub the purée through a sieve with the back of a ladle or a wooden spoon.

3   Store the purée in a tightly covered jar in the fridge. It will keep for a few days.

dressings

classic vinaigrette

Sometimes a simple light dressing is all that is needed to enhance the subtle flavours of grilled, pan-roasted or steamed fish. Used to dress flaked fish and salad leaves, it also forms an integral part of a light starter or main course. My recipe for vinaigrette uses sherry vinegar, to give the dressing a good depth of flavour. Mixing several oils keeps the consistency light.

Makes 350ml

50ml sherry vinegar

125ml extra-virgin olive oil

125ml olive oil

50ml groundnut oil

1 tbsp fresh lemon juice

sea salt and freshly ground black pepper

Simply whisk all the ingredients together in a bowl or jug to form a light emulsion. Season with a good pinch each of salt and pepper and serve. Store the vinaigrette in a screw-top glass jar, and shake before using.

lemon grass vinaigrette

1 stalk fresh lemon grass

2 tbsp olive oil

350ml Classic Vinaigrette (above)

Split the stalk of lemon grass in half, then chop finely. Warm the oil gently and add the lemon grass. Leave to infuse for 3–4 hours. Strain the oil and mix into the vinaigrette.

shallot and herb vinaigrette

1 medium shallot, finely chopped

1 tbsp chopped fresh herbs (e.g. basil, tarragon and chervil)

350ml Classic Vinaigrette (left)

Mix the shallot with the herbs and stir into the vinaigrette.

hazelnut vinaigrette

Substitute hazelnut oil for the extra-virgin olive oil in the Classic Vinaigrette recipe (left).

caviar vinaigrette

175ml Classic Vinaigrette (left)

1 tbsp caviar

Make up the vinaigrette and whisk in the caviar just before serving.

cream vinaigrette

This vinaigrette, enriched and thickened with double cream, can be used to dress salad leaves, hot baby vegetables or simple poached or steamed fish.

Makes 280ml

150ml extra-virgin olive oil

50ml groundnut oil

2 tbsp sherry vinegar

50ml double cream

sea salt and freshly ground black pepper

In a bowl or jug, whisk together the oils and vinegar. Lightly whip the cream, then fold into the dressing. Season well with salt and pepper and serve.

mustard cream vinaigrette

2 tbsp Pommery mustard or other whole-grained mustard

280ml Cream Vinaigrette (above)

Simply whisk the mustard into the cream vinaigrette.

dill and sweet mustard cream vinaigrette

280ml Cream Vinaigrette (above)

1 tbsp chopped fresh dill

2 tbsp honey mustard, or 4 tsp Pommery or whole-grained mustard

Make up the cream vinaigrette and whisk in the dill and mustard.

from front: lemon grass vinaigrette, shallot and herb vinaigrette, classic vinaigrette

soups

Fish and shellfish are synonymous with a chowder. This particular example makes a great family soup which we often enjoy at weekends: it is especially welcoming on a cold, wet Sunday.

chowder belle-mère

Serves 4–6

1 tbsp olive oil

70g cooking pancetta or streaky bacon, de-rinded and chopped

25g butter

1 onion, thinly sliced

1 medium potato, peeled and chopped

1 litre Chicken Stock (page 61) or Fish Stock (pages 58–59)

200g undyed smoked haddock fillet, skinned and chopped

200g cod or haddock fillet, skinned and chopped

250g sweetcorn, fresh or frozen

120g cooked peeled prawns, thawed if frozen

2 tbsp double cream (optional)

dash or two Tabasco (optional)

1 tbsp chopped fresh parsley

sea salt and freshly ground black pepper

Alternative fish: coley, whiting

Recommended drinks: mineral water or a light tisane such as linden leaf, vervaine or green leaf tea

1   In a large saucepan, heat the oil and gently sauté the chopped pancetta or bacon for about 5 minutes until crispy but not brown. Drain off the oil and set the pancetta aside on kitchen paper towel.

2   Melt the butter in the same pan. Add the onion and potato and heat until they start to sizzle. Cook gently for about 5 minutes until softened.

3   Return the pancetta to the pan, pour in the stock and bring to the boil. Simmer uncovered for 12 minutes or until the potato is softened. Stir in all of the chopped fish and simmer for about 5 minutes.

4   Add the sweetcorn and prawns and cook for a further 3 minutes. By now the fish should be flaky and the soup lightly thickened. Stir in the cream, if using, and season to taste. If you want a hot, spicy flavour, add one or two dashes of Tabasco at this point. Mix in the parsley and serve.

Prawns and mango make a surprisingly good combination. This soup works well as a first course because you can make it in advance and then reheat it. You can use either raw tiger prawns or cooked cold-water prawns. Make sure the mango is perfectly ripe to ensure a good balance of flavours.

prawn and mango mulligatawny

1   In a large saucepan, heat the oil and stir in the carrots, onion, leek, celery, garlic and potato. Sauté gently for 5 minutes until softened. Chop half the prawns and add to the pan together with the curry powder, saffron strands and chopped tomatoes. Cook for another 5 minutes.

2   Meanwhile, pour 200ml of water into another saucepan. Add the rice and bring to the boil. Lower to a simmer, cover and cook gently for 10 minutes. Remove from the heat without lifting the lid and set aside.

3   Pour the stock into the pan with the vegetables and prawns. Bring to the boil, then lower to a simmer and cook gently for 15 minutes. Remove from the heat and allow the soup to cool a little.

4   Pour the soup into a food processor or blender and whizz until very smooth, scraping down the sides of the container once or twice. Pass through a sieve, rubbing with the back of a ladle or a wooden spoon.

5   Return the soup to the pan. Mix in the rice and mango and bring to a gentle simmer. Meanwhile, if using tiger prawns, split the remaining prawns in half lengthways. Add to the pan. Cook for 3 minutes, then stir in the cream. If the soup is too thick, add a little boiling water to thin it down. Season, and serve hot, sprinkled with the parsley.

Serves 4–6

2 tbsp olive oil

2 medium carrots, finely chopped

1 small onion, finely chopped

1 medium leek, white only, finely
    chopped

1 celery stick, finely chopped

1 large clove garlic, crushed

1 medium potato, peeled and
    finely chopped

300g raw tiger prawns or cooked
    cold-water prawns, peeled

1 tsp mild curry powder

good pinch saffron strands

300g plum tomatoes, skinned,
    de-seeded and chopped

100g basmati rice

1.2 litres Fish Stock (pages 58–59)

½ small ripe mango, finely chopped

4 tbsp single cream

sea salt and freshly ground black pepper

2 tsp finely chopped fresh parsley

Alternative fish: crab, scallops

Recommended wines: Condrieu
    'La Doriane', Etienne Guigal

A fragrant, creamy soup, this contains cubes of pan-fried cod to add flavour and texture. The distinct aniseed flavour of fennel is cleverly enhanced with a hint of star anise, and perfectly contrasts with the delicate taste of the fish. Slices of warm walnut bread make a delicious accompaniment.

fennel soup with pan-roasted cod

Serves 4

2 tbsp olive oil

1 large shallot, chopped

1 large bulb fennel, chopped

4 star anise

100ml dry white wine

1 litre Fish Stock (pages 58–59)

100ml double cream

2 tsp chopped fresh dill

200g cod fillet, skinned and cut into
   1cm cubes

sea salt and freshly ground black pepper

Alternative fish: haddock, hake, whiting

Recommended drinks: mineral water,
   Manzanilla sherry or a light unoaked
   Chardonnay, e.g. Chablis premier cru

1   In a large saucepan, heat half the olive oil, then gently sauté the shallot and fennel with the star anise for about 10 minutes until softened but not coloured. Pour in the wine and cook for about 5 minutes until well reduced and almost syrupy. Pour in the stock, season and bring to the boil. Cover the pan and reduce the heat. Simmer gently for about 25 minutes.

2   Remove the star anise and stir in the cream. Simmer, uncovered, for about 3 minutes. Pour into a food processor and whizz until smooth. Pass the purée through a sieve set over a bowl, rubbing with the back of a ladle or a wooden spoon. Pour back into the pan and season to taste. Stir in the dill. Reheat the soup gently, if necessary, and keep warm.

3   In a non-stick frying pan, heat the remaining oil until it just starts to smoke. Cook the cubes of cod, without stirring, until golden brown on the base. Carefully turn them over and cook on the other side for 1–2 minutes to brown. Take care not to overcook. Season the fish lightly.

4   Ladle the soup into four warmed soup plates and spoon the browned cubes of cod into the centre. Serve straight away.

A great meal of a soup, this is full of Italian spirit and liveliness. You should be able to buy most of the fish from a well-stocked fishmonger. If not, then replace any unavailable fish with equivalents or leave them out altogether. The soup is excellent served with croûtons made from slices of baguette.

classic italian fish soup

Serves 8

400g fresh sardines

1 dorade royale (gilt-head bream),
 about 650g

1 small red mullet

200g monkfish tail, filleted

200g baby squid, prepared

2 pinches saffron strands

100ml extra-virgin olive oil

300g fresh mussels, de-bearded

200g fresh cockles, scrubbed

1 small onion, chopped

2 large cloves garlic, chopped

2 tbsp chopped bulb fennel

1 large celery stick, chopped

250g ripe plum tomatoes, skinned,
 de-seeded and chopped

2 tsp tomato purée

sprigs fresh parsley and thyme

2 each fresh sage and bay leaves

4 tsp Cognac or other brandy

200ml Italian dry white wine

sprigs fresh basil

sea salt and freshly ground black pepper

Recommended wine: Pinot Grigio

1   If necessary, scale and gut the whole fish, then remove the heads, fins and gills and discard. Chop all the fish into chunks. Cut up the squid if large. Mix the fish and squid with half the saffron strands and half the olive oil and set aside.

2   Heat a large saucepan filled with just enough water to cover the bottom and add the mussels and cockles. Bring to the boil, then cover and cook over a gentle heat for a few minutes until the shells open. Discard any unopened shells, then set the rest aside until cool enough to handle. Drain, saving the pan juices for later. Remove the flesh from the shells and set aside; discard the shells.

3   Add the remaining oil to the pan with the onion, garlic, fennel, celery, tomatoes and tomato purée, and stir. Heat until sizzling, then reduce the heat. Cover and cook for about 10 minutes until the vegetables are lightly browned and softened.

4   Tie the parsley, thyme, sage and bay leaves together with kitchen string and add to the pan. Next, add the fish and squid and cook, stirring, until lightly coloured. Mix in the brandy and cook for a further 2 minutes. Pour in the wine and simmer until all the liquid has evaporated.

5   Pour in about 1.5 litres of water, or just enough to cover, and add the mussels and cockles with their reserved pan juices. Bring to the boil. Season and add 2 large basil sprigs. Cover and simmer gently for about 20 minutes. As the fish softens, break down the flesh with a wooden spoon. Remove from the heat and allow to cool for 20 minutes or so.

6   Remove the bundle of herbs, then blend the soup in a food processor until smooth. You will have to do this in batches. Pass the purée through a large sieve set over a big bowl or saucepan, rubbing with the back of a ladle or a wooden spoon. Discard any bones and vegetable debris that cannot be passed through the sieve. Gently reheat the soup and check the seasoning. Garnish with a few fresh basil leaves and serve at once.

When mussels are cheap and plentiful, this is a nice hearty soup to make for a light lunch or supper, served with chunks of fresh crusty bread. There's no need to make fish stock first as this forms part of the recipe. A mirepoix – a mixture of finely chopped vegetables – infuses the soup with its subtle, delicate flavour.

mussel soup with coriander

1   Melt the butter in a large saucepan. Add the onion and wine and cook until bubbling. Tip in the mussels, cover with a well-fitting lid and reduce the heat to low. Cook for 5–7 minutes, shaking the pan gently once or twice, until the shells open. Discard any mussels that are still closed. Drain into a bowl and reserve the juices and shellfish separately. When cool enough to handle, remove the meat from the shells and set aside. Discard the shells and onion.

2   Heat the oil in the same saucepan and add the shallot, carrot, leek, fennel and garlic (the mirepoix) together with the thyme, coriander seeds and saffron. Cover and cook gently for about 5 minutes. Add the tomatoes and potato, cover again and sweat down for another 5 minutes. Add the Pernod and cook, uncovered, for a minute or two until the liquid has completely evaporated. Pour in the vermouth and continue cooking until reduced by half.

3   Stir in the reserved mussel juices, half the mussels and 750ml of water. Season lightly. Bring to the boil, then cover and simmer for 15 minutes. Remove from the heat. Discard the thyme, then add the chopped fresh coriander and leave to infuse for approximately 5 minutes.

4   Pour the mixture into a food processor and blend until smooth. Pass through a sieve into another pan, rubbing with the back of a ladle or a wooden spoon. (If the soup seems rather too thick, thin it down with a little water.) Add the rest of the cooked mussels and reheat gently. Check the seasoning and serve.

Serves 4

25g butter

3–4 slices of onion

4 tbsp dry white wine

1kg fresh mussels, scrubbed
    and de-bearded

2 tbsp olive oil

1 shallot, finely chopped

1 carrot, finely diced

1 leek, white only, finely diced

½ small bulb fennel, finely diced

2 large cloves garlic, finely chopped

1 sprig fresh thyme

½ tsp crushed coriander seeds

good pinch saffron strands

2 medium plum tomatoes, skinned,
    de-seeded and chopped

1 small potato, peeled and finely diced

1 tbsp Pernod

100ml Noilly Prat or other dry vermouth

1 tbsp chopped fresh coriander

sea salt and freshly ground black pepper

Recommended wines: Californian or
    Australian Chardonnay

An exotic soup brimming with the flavours of the Orient, this is spiked with aromatic harissa spice paste. You can buy palm sugar in Asian food stores but, if you can't find it, then use light soft brown sugar instead. I make my own pickled ginger by cooking thin slices of fresh ginger in vivid pink grenadine. However, you can use the Japanese pickled ginger sold in Oriental supermarkets to go with sushi, if you don't have the time to make your own. I urge you to try this soup as it is bound to get your guests talking.

hot and sour tiger prawn broth

1   Wrap the lemon grass in a small piece of muslin and tie with kitchen string. Place the muslin bag in a large saucepan with the oil, garlic and harissa. Heat until sizzling, then cook gently for about 5 minutes.

2   Add the chillies, ginger, sugar and coriander and cook for another 5 minutes. Pour in the stock and add the lime zest and juice. Sprinkle in a little salt to season. Bring to the boil and simmer for 5 minutes.

3   Strain the broth, discarding the muslin bag and spices, and return to the pan. Add the prawns, then bring to the boil and simmer for 2 minutes. Add the asparagus, peas and broad beans and simmer for another 2 minutes. Adjust the seasoning, if necessary. Sprinkle the shredded basil over the broth and serve.

Serves 4–6

3 stalks fresh lemon grass, finely sliced

1 tbsp olive oil

1 large clove garlic, chopped

1 tsp Fresh Harissa (page 70)

1 large fresh red chilli, de-seeded and finely sliced

1 large fresh green chilli, de-seeded and finely sliced

2 tsp pickled ginger

2 tsp palm sugar or light soft brown sugar

1 tbsp chopped fresh coriander leaves

1 litre Chicken Stock (page 61)

grated zest and juice 2 limes

400g peeled raw tiger prawns

12 asparagus tips

2 tbsp shelled peas

2 tbsp shelled baby broad beans

1 tbsp shredded fresh basil

sea salt and freshly ground black pepper

Recommended wines: Côte du Lubéron Rosé

Crab and sweetcorn make natural partners because of their equally distinctive sweet flavours. This soup is made in the Cajun style: thickened with a classic roux, well cooked out for good flavour, and then served with chilli-flavoured crab and sweetcorn patties. Fresh crab deserves fresh sweetcorn, but frozen will do.

crab and sweetcorn soup with crab cakes

Serves 6

1 large cooked crab

6 corn on the cobs

1 litre Chicken Stock (page 61)

100g butter

1 large onion, chopped

50g flour + 2 tbsp for coating

500ml milk

3 tbsp olive oil

1 small fresh green chilli, de-seeded and
   very finely chopped

30g fresh breadcrumbs

1 small egg white, lightly beaten

½ tsp mild chilli powder

sprigs fresh flat-leaf parsley or coriander
   to serve

sea salt and freshly ground black pepper

Recommended wine: New Zealand
   Sauvignon Blanc

1   Remove about 125g white meat from the crab and set aside in a bowl. Remove the remaining white and brown meat; reserve in another bowl. Keep the crab shell.

2   Remove the husks and 'silk' from the corn on the cobs (reserve the husks). Grate the kernels from one of the cobs, then press in a small sieve to extract the milky juice. Reserve the flesh and juice separately. Cut the kernels off the other cobs. Set aside.

3   In a large saucepan, combine the stock, corn husks, reserved corn juice and crab shell and bring to the boil. Reduce the heat and simmer for about 15 minutes. Strain the stock into a bowl or jug and discard the husks and shell.

4   Melt the butter in the pan and gently sauté the onion for about 5 minutes, or until softened. Stir in the 50g of flour. Cook for 2 minutes or until the roux is a light golden colour. Gradually pour in the reserved stock and the milk, stirring until smooth. Season well and bring to the boil. Stir in the ungrated sweetcorn kernels and the mixed brown and white crab meat. Simmer for 10 minutes, stirring occasionally.

5   Meanwhile, make the crab cakes. In a small saucepan, heat 1 teaspoon of the oil and gently fry the green chilli for 2–3 minutes until softened. Add the chilli to the white crab meat together with the grated sweetcorn, breadcrumbs, ½ teaspoon salt, some pepper and just enough egg white to form a firm mixture. Shape into 6 small neat patties and toss in the 2 tablespoons of flour to coat evenly.

6   In a small frying pan, heat 2 tablespoons of the remaining oil and fry the patties for about 3 minutes on each side, or until golden brown and just firm. Remove and keep warm. Wipe out the pan with a kitchen paper towel. Heat the remaining oil in it with the chilli powder for a minute or two until well blended. Keep warm.

7   Blend the soup in a food processor until smooth, then pass through a sieve into a clean saucepan, rubbing with the back of a ladle or a wooden spoon. Check the seasoning, then return to a gentle boil. Pour the soup into six warmed, shallow soup plates. Place a crab cake in the middle of each bowl and trickle over the chilli oil. Garnish with the parsley or coriander and serve immediately.

This unusual and refreshing soup, with its plump lobster pieces and palate-cleansing chunks of melon, is popular in the South of France. If served in small cups with dainty spoons, it makes an elegant starter on a summer's evening. Be sure to use well-flavoured ripe melons and to chill the soup well before serving.

chilled melon and lobster soup

1   In a large bowl, mix together the melon, shredded basil, lime zest, Pernod and orange juice. Stir well, then cover and chill for at least 6 hours, or overnight, if possible.

2   Purée the chilled fruit and liquid in a food processor, then pass it through a sieve, pressing with the back of a ladle or a wooden spoon. Chill in the freezer for a good half hour while preparing the lobster, or leave it in the fridge overnight.

3   Mix the lobster with the vinaigrette and set aside to marinate for half an hour.

4   Spoon the lobster into six bowls. Stir the lime juice into the melon soup and pour over the lobster. Garnish with the fresh basil leaves and serve straight away.

Serves 6

¼ small ripe watermelon, about 800g, de-seeded and finely diced

2 ripe Ogen melons, de-seeded and finely diced

10g fresh basil leaves, roughly shredded + small leaves to garnish

grated zest and juice 1 lime

1 tsp Pernod

100ml freshly squeezed orange juice

200g cooked lobster meat, chopped into small pieces

1 tbsp Classic Vinaigrette (page 76)

Alternative fish: cooked langoustines, tiger prawns

Recommended wines: chilled white port or Pinot Blanc

This colourful soup is particularly suitable for a light lunch with friends. The prawns make it a popular treat but, for a subtle change of flavour, you can use small chunks of monkfish. The soup is a warming choice for winter, but easily converts to a summer dish if you leave out the bacon, cabbage and mushrooms.

pistou soup with prawns

Serves 4–6

18 raw langoustines or tiger prawns

2 tbsp olive oil

1 small potato, peeled and finely diced

2 medium carrots, finely diced

1 medium courgette, finely diced

1 medium leek, finely sliced

1 small onion, finely chopped

1 large clove garlic, crushed

100g smoked back bacon, de-rinded
   and cut into thin strips

100g cooked haricot beans

100g wild mushrooms, preferably
   light-coloured ones, sliced

1 litre Chicken Stock (page 61), Fish
   Stock (pages 58–59) or Vegetable
   Nage (page 61)

100g Savoy or other green cabbage,
   finely shredded

3–4 large leaves fresh basil, shredded

2–4 tsp Fresh Pesto (page 75)

sea salt and freshly ground black pepper

Alternative fish: monkfish

Recommended drink: a light beer or
   lager, well chilled

1   Peel the langoustines or prawns and set aside. In a large saucepan, heat the oil, then stir in the potato, carrots, courgette, leek, onion, garlic and bacon. Gently sizzle for about 10 minutes, stirring occasionally. Add the beans and mushrooms and cook for 5 minutes. Stir in the stock, season and bring to the boil. Reduce the heat and simmer for 10 minutes.

2   Meanwhile, blanch the cabbage in a little boiling water for no more than a minute. Drain and refresh in cold water, then set aside.

3   Add the langoustines or prawns to the simmering soup and cook for 2 minutes. Stir in the cabbage and shredded basil leaves. Reheat until just on the point of boiling, and check the seasoning.

4   To serve, use two teaspoons to shape the pesto into small quenelles. Ladle the soup into warmed bowls and slip a quenelle into the centre of each one.

starters

The Spanish and Mexicans have a way of marinating fish in a spiced dressing immediately after it has been cooked. The fish bask in a balsamic vinegar and olive oil dressing, absorbing the flavours of saffron, coriander and star anise. The dish is then served at room temperature to make the most of all its wonderful flavours.

escabèche of sardines

Serves 4

6 x 300g sardines, whole or filleted,
  with skin on

100ml olive oil

1 large shallot, thinly sliced

1 medium carrot, thinly sliced

½ tsp coriander seeds, lightly crushed

1 whole star anise

good pinch saffron strands

1 tsp white wine vinegar

1 tsp balsamic vinegar

chopped fresh parsley to garnish

sea salt and freshly ground black pepper

Alternative fish: red mullet

Recommended wines: an Alsace
  Riesling or white Provençal Cassis

1   This recipe is easiest made with simple fillets of sardine. However, should you wish to serve the fish as butterfly fillets, have your fishmonger gut and clean the fish as normal. Remove the heads and fins. Slit the fish wide open down the belly side and lay, spread out, on a board, flesh side down. Press down firmly on the backbone, then turn the fish over and pull out the whole skeleton with your fingers, snipping it at the tail (leave the tail on if you wish). The skeleton should come away easily. If using fillets, trim the edges and pull out any pin bones you find. Season the fish. Heat a non-stick pan until just smoking, then add 2 tablespoons of the oil and heat again. Fry the fish, skin side down, for about 2 minutes. Flip them over and cook for 2 more minutes, or until just cooked. Transfer to a serving dish and allow to cool.

2   Wipe out the pan and heat half the remaining oil. Gently sauté the shallot and carrot with the coriander, star anise and saffron for about 5 minutes, or until softened.

3   Add the two vinegars and the remaining oil. Bring to the boil and check the seasoning. Spoon over the fish, making sure they are all equally covered. Leave to cool to room temperature. Sprinkle over a little chopped parsley before serving.

Homemade salt cod has a sweeter aroma than the pungent ready-prepared version. It can be cooked in the same way as fresh cod – poached, steamed or pan-fried – but avoid grilling as this tends to toughen the flesh. It also makes delicious fishcakes. A brandade is usually finely flaked fish mixed with potato, but mine combines fish with cream and leeks. You need to start preparing this dish about 24 hours ahead of serving.

brandade of homemade salt cod

Serves 8

For the salt cod:

handful fresh parsley stalks, chopped

100g sea salt flakes

1 x 500g thick fresh cod fillet, skinned
   and pin boned

For the mousse:

50g unsalted butter

1 medium onion, finely chopped

1 medium leek, finely shredded

500ml double cream

2 leaves gelatine or 1⅓ tsp
   gelatine crystals

freshly ground white pepper (optional)

Recommended wines: an Alsace
   Pinot Blanc or Pinot Grigio

1   Mix the parsley stalks and salt and scatter half of the mixture in the centre of a shallow dish, just big enough to hold the cod. Press the fish, skinned side down, into the salt and pat the remaining mixture on top. Cover with cling film, then lightly weight the fish with a plate or flat dish placed on top. Take care not to flatten the fish with too heavy a weight. Refrigerate for 24 hours.

2   Remove the cod from the fridge and drain off the exuded liquid. Rinse off the salt and parsley under cold running water, then pat dry with kitchen paper towels. Cut the fish into small chunks.

3   Melt the butter in a sauté pan and add the onion and leek. Cover and sweat very gently for about 10 minutes, shaking the pan occasionally. If possible, do not remove the lid or you will let out the steam. Stir in the diced cod and cook uncovered for a further 5 minutes, stirring once or twice. Pour in half the cream and bring to a gentle boil, then cook, uncovered, until reduced by half. Season with white pepper, if using.

4   Blend the fish mixture in a food processor until very smooth, scraping the sides of the container down once or twice. (For extra smoothness, pass through a fine sieve, rubbing with a plastic scraper or the back of a ladle.)

5   Next, put the gelatine leaves in a bowl and cover with cold water. When soft, drain the leaves and squeeze out excess moisture, then put them back in the bowl. Either set the bowl over a pan of simmering water to melt the gelatine, stirring once or twice, or heat in a microwave oven on full power for up to 1 minute. (If using gelatine crystals, dissolve in 2 tablespoons of boiling water, stirring briskly.) Quickly mix the gelatine into the cooling cod mixture. Chill for about 1–2 hours, or until beginning to set.

6   Whip the remaining cream into soft floppy peaks. Gently fold into the cod mixture with a large metal spoon. Check the seasoning. Spoon into 8 ramekin dishes. Cover and refrigerate once again until set. Serve with triangles of hot toast or melba toast.

This recipe is worlds away from the classic fried skate with capers and mash. Ramekin dishes are lined with strips of poached skate, then filled with a mixture of capers, gherkins and parsley gelatine stock and left to set. These are served with a rousse garnish – a mixture of baby carrots and onions – and Sauce Gribiche.

skate and parsley moulds

1   First, make the rousse garnish: run a canelle knife down the sides of the carrots, then slice across to form daisy shapes. Bring the court-bouillon to the boil in a wide saucepan. Add the carrots and onions and blanch for 2 minutes. Remove with a slotted spoon and transfer to a bowl. Toss with the vinaigrette and set aside.

2   Reheat the court-bouillon to a gentle simmer. Submerge the skate wings in it, making sure they are completely covered, and poach for 5–7 minutes until the flesh seems just firm. Remove from the heat and allow the skate to cool in the liquid.

3   Meanwhile, soak the gelatine leaves in cold water until softened, then drain and squeeze out the excess moisture. Return the gelatine to the bowl. Heat the fish stock to boiling, then pour through a sieve lined with wet muslin or a clean J-cloth into the bowl containing the gelatine. Stir until melted. (If you are using gelatine crystals, sprinkle them on to the just-boiled liquid, stirring until dissolved.) Stir in the chopped parsley and set aside to cool.

4   When the fish has cooled to room temperature, remove it from the liquid and peel off the skin. Take the flesh from the bones in long strips (you should have about 600g of flesh). Save the court-bouillon; it can be strained and reused.

5   Now build the moulds: pour a dribble of parsley stock into each mould to cover the bottom. Sprinkle on a few chopped gherkins and capers and leave to set until firm. When the bases have set, wind the strips of skate around the insides of the moulds, scattering gherkins and capers in the centre as you go. When you reach the top, pour over the remaining parsley stock. Gently tap the moulds on the work surface to make sure there are no air gaps. Stand the moulds on a plate, cover and carefully transfer to the fridge. Leave to set for at least 12 hours.

6   To serve, dip the moulds in very hot water for a few seconds, then turn out on to plates, loosening the sides with a table knife, if necessary. Serve with the rousse garnish and sauce gribiche.

Serves 6

250g baby carrots, scrubbed
2 litres Court-bouillon (page 58)
125g baby onions, sliced
2 tbsp Classic Vinaigrette (page 76)
1kg medium skate wings
7 leaves gelatine or
   4 tsp gelatine crystals
500ml Fish Stock (pages 58–59)
4 tbsp finely chopped fresh parsley
2 tbsp chopped gherkins
2 tbsp chopped capers
300ml Sauce Gribiche (page 69)
   to serve

Alternative fish: sole
Recommended wine: an American
   Fumé Blanc

Fish terrines present an opportunity to create a work of art on a plate, yet are surprisingly simple to make. The secret of their success is to be well prepared before you start cooking. It also helps to use the classic sized terrine mould, long and narrow, about 22 x 8cm, with a 1 litre capacity. Traditional loaf tins will do, but their extra width makes it tricky to remove slices from the tin without any breakages.

red mullet and pepper terrine

1   In a bowl, soak the gelatine leaves in a little cold water until softened, then drain and squeeze out excess moisture. Return the gelatine to the bowl. Heat the stock in a saucepan to boiling. Strain it through a fine sieve lined with wet muslin or a clean J-cloth into the bowl containing the gelatine and stir until the gelatine has melted. (If you are using gelatine crystals, sprinkle them on to the just-boiled stock and stir briskly until dissolved.) Stir in the tarragon and set aside to cool.

2   Using a wide swivel vegetable peeler, remove the skin from the peppers, then halve, core and trim away the inside ribs. Cut the flesh into fine, long strips. Remove any pin bones from the fish using tweezers, if necessary.

3   Heat 2 tablespoons of the oil in a large non-stick frying pan and sauté the peppers for about 10 minutes, or until they are softened but not browned. Remove and drain on a kitchen paper towel. Wipe out the pan and heat the remaining oil to almost smoking. Cook the fish fillets, skin side down, for 2 minutes. Flip them over and cook for another 2 minutes, then remove and season both sides.

4   Now assemble your terrine: first, line the mould with cling film, allowing a generous overhang. The fish fillets should just fit inside without having to be trimmed. Lay 2 fillets, skin side down, lengthways on the bottom. Fill in the gaps and cover the fish with half of the pepper strips, seasoning as you go. Pour over enough of the setting stock just to cover the first layer, and tap the terrine gently to make sure there are no air gaps. Repeat with the remaining fish and peppers and more stock, enough just to submerge the pepper strips. Fold the cling film over the top and chill until set.

5   To serve, dip the base of the mould in a bowl of just-boiled water for a few seconds, then run a table knife around the outside of the terrine. Shake out on to a board and peel off the cling film. Cut into slices, preferably with an electric carving knife, or a serrated knife. Garnish with the chervil sprigs and serve.

Serves 6

7 leaves gelatine, or
    4 tsp gelatine crystals
500ml Fish Stock (pages 58–59)
1 tbsp chopped fresh tarragon
3 large yellow peppers
3 large red peppers
4 x 120g red mullet fillets, skin on
3 tbsp olive oil
sprigs fresh chervil to garnish
sea salt and freshly ground black pepper

Alternative fish: salmon fillets
Recommended wines: a white
    Provençal Palette or a red Anjou

Most fish pâtés are smooth, but this duck and salmon pâté has a rougher texture, imitating the French pots of shredded meat combined with duck fat. Next time you roast a duck, pour off the fat and save it for this dish. A medium to large duck will give you enough fat for the recipe. Otherwise, the fat from five medium duck breasts will produce the same amount. For a light summer version of this dish, fold in some crème fraîche and vinaigrette after adding the coriander, and shape into quenelles.

salmon rillettes

Serves 4–6

500g skinned fresh salmon fillet

250ml duck fat, strained

2 tbsp chopped fresh coriander + baby
   coriander sprigs to garnish

sea salt and freshly ground black pepper

Recommended wines: Savennières or
   a light Pinot Noir

1   Remove any pin bones from the salmon and make sure there is no dark blood line on the underside of the fish. Cut into chunks. Melt the duck fat in a saucepan until just below 100°C/212°F.

2   Add the salmon to the hot fat and poach very gently for 5 minutes. The chunks of fish should turn a very pale pink. Gently shake the pan once or twice as they cook. Remove the pan from the heat and allow the fish to stand in the fat for another 5 minutes. When ready, the fish should just flake but still be very slightly darker pink in the centre of the chunks.

3   Using a draining spoon, transfer the fish to a bowl and flake finely with a fork. Mix in about 2–3 tablespoons of the duck fat. Season to taste with salt and pepper, then leave to cool.

4   Stir in the chopped coriander and spoon into small ramekins. Garnish each with a sprig or two of coriander. Chill for about 1 hour, or until lightly firm.

Fishmongers often sell ready-cooked lobster, and a single specimen can be stretched to feed four or more with this light and summery terrine. Cooked chunks of salmon fillet work equally well. Serve with a creamy tomato sauce and a salad dressed with a hazelnut vinaigrette (page 76).

lobster and provençal vegetable terrine

1   Prepare the cooked lobster and extract the meat, keeping it in bite-sized chunks. Set the meat aside. In a large saucepan, combine the lobster shell with the fish stock and boil for about 15 minutes to extract the flavour. Check the stock for seasoning, then strain through a muslin-lined sieve and return to the saucepan.

2   Blanch the courgettes and peppers in a pan of boiling water for a minute or less, until just softened. Drain and refresh in ice-cold water. Drain again and pat dry with kitchen paper towels.

3   Cover the gelatine leaves with cold water and soak until just softened. Drain and squeeze dry. Reheat the stock until boiling, then pour on to the gelatine leaves and stir until melted. (If using gelatine crystals, sprinkle them on to the just-boiling stock and stir briskly until dissolved.) Stir in the chopped tarragon and chervil. Set the stock aside until cool, but not set.

4   Now make your terrine: line a 1 litre terrine mould, 22 x 8cm, with cling film, allowing an overhang. Scatter some of the diced courgettes and peppers over the bottom. Arrange the lobster chunks and tomatoes on top, scattering more diced courgettes and peppers in between. Pour in a little stock and tap the mould gently to make sure there are no air holes.

5   Repeat with the rest of the lobster, tomatoes and diced courgettes and peppers. When you have filled the terrine, pour on enough stock to submerge the ingredients. Fold over the cling film, then chill for at least 12 hours or until firm.

6   To turn out, dip the mould briefly in a bowl of boiling water, then tip out on to a cutting board. Using a serrated knife or electric carving knife, cut into thick slices. Lift the slices on to serving plates with a fish slice. Serve with the olives, a dressed salad and the sauce gazpacho.

Serves 6

1 large lobster (about 1 kg), cooked
500ml Fish Stock (pages 58–59)
4 medium courgettes, finely diced
2 red peppers, finely diced
2 yellow peppers, finely diced
7 leaves gelatine, or
  4 tsp gelatine crystals
2 tbsp chopped fresh tarragon
2 tbsp chopped fresh chervil
4 firm plum tomatoes, skinned,
  quartered and de-seeded
2 tbsp finely chopped black olives
300ml Sauce Gazpacho (page 69)
sea salt and freshly ground
  black pepper

Alternative fish: salmon
Recommended wine: Chassagne-
  Montrachet premier cru

A recipe that is simplicity itself. It could be a starter (allow 3 per head), a light lunch or – made in miniature – served as canapés. Crab and sweetcorn are encased in rice paper wrappers or filo pastry and fried. If using filo pastry, keep the sheets covered with cling film while working, to stop them drying out.

crab and sweetcorn spring rolls

Serves 4

300g white crab meat

3 tbsp Mustard Mayonnaise (page 66)

100g cooked sweetcorn, patted dry

1 tbsp chopped fresh basil

1 tbsp chopped fresh coriander

12 rice paper wrappers or sheets of filo
   pastry (each about 23cm square)

2 egg yolks, beaten with 1 tsp water

100ml Classic Vinaigrette (page 76)

1 tbsp Fresh Harissa (page 70)

sunflower oil for deep-frying

salad leaves to serve (optional)

sea salt and freshly ground black pepper

Alternative fish: lobster

Recommended wines: a New Zealand
   Sauvignon Blanc or Pinot Grigio

1   Finely flake the crab meat with a fork, removing any stray pieces of shell or cartilage as you go. Season well and mix with the mustard mayonnaise, sweetcorn, basil and coriander.

2   Place a rice paper wrapper or a sheet of filo at an angle on a board so that one of the corners points towards you. Brush around the edges with the egg-yolk wash. Spoon about a tablespoon of the crab filling in a line near the top corner. Fold over the top corner and roll towards you a little, then fold in the sides and continue to roll up. Place on a non-stick tray. Repeat with the remaining filling, wrappers or filo, and egg wash to make 12 rolls in all. Lightly brush with the remaining egg wash and chill for about 30 minutes.

3   Meanwhile, whisk the vinaigrette with the harissa and set aside.

4   Pour oil to a depth of 6–7cm into a deep pan and heat to a temperature of around 180°C/350°F, or until a small piece of white bread turns golden brown in about 30 seconds. Deep-fry the rolls, four at a time, for 3–4 minutes or until golden brown and crisp on all sides. Reheat the oil in between batches. Drain on kitchen paper towels. Serve warm and crisp, with the harissa vinaigrette as a dipping sauce. A little salad goes well with this, but is not essential.

This recipe uses raw scallops in their freshest glory. For the best results, buy scallops that are still enclosed in shells, and ask your fishmonger to open and clean them for you if you are not so inclined. Then make this recipe the same day. Serve on a bed of sliced cucumber or spoon into their shells and serve as canapés.

tartare of scallops and smoked salmon

Serves 4

12 large fresh scallops, shelled, trimmed
  and cleaned
150g oak-smoked salmon
2 tbsp crème fraîche
1 tbsp fresh lime juice
1 tbsp chopped fresh chives
1 tbsp chopped fresh chervil + extra
  chervil to garnish
½ cucumber, sliced wafer thin, to serve
sea salt and freshly ground black pepper

Recommended wines: Riesling or
  Terre di Tuffi

1   Cut the scallops and smoked salmon into very small, even dice, then season well. Mix in the crème fraîche, lime juice, chives and chervil. Keep in the fridge.

2   About 15 minutes before serving, shape the mixture. Stretch cling film over a large plate until taut. This will make the tartares easier to remove. Working on the cling film, press one-quarter of the fish mixture into a plain round biscuit cutter. Lift off the cutter, leaving the shaped tartare on the cling film. Repeat with the remaining tartare, to shape three more rounds. Chill in the freezer for about 15 minutes.

3   Meanwhile, season the thin slices of cucumber and arrange them on four serving plates. Remove the chilled fish from the freezer. Using a fish slice, scoop each round of tartare off the cling film and place on the cucumber on each serving plate. Garnish each serving with a wisp of chervil.

Variation

If you feel eating raw scallops is a little too brave, then by all means lightly pan-fry them first. Heat a non-stick pan lightly coated with a little olive oil until hot and fry the scallops for just a minute on each side. Allow to cool, then proceed with the recipe. Pan-frying gives the scallops a tangy caramelized flavour.

A hot, fresh salmon mousse makes a simple but sophisticated starter which can be prepared ahead and baked just before serving. The light texture is achieved by folding in the whipped cream over a bowl of crushed ice. A simpler way is to fold well-chilled cream into the fish in a freezer-chilled bowl.

hot salmon mousse

1   Whizz the salmon in a food processor or blender until very smooth, scraping down the sides of the container as necessary. (Be prepared to blend for quite a long while.) Season with the salt and white pepper, if using, and mix in the lemon juice. For the ultimate in lightness, pass the mixture through a fine sieve, rubbing with a plastic scraper. Scoop the mixture into a large mixing bowl. Fill an even larger bowl with crushed ice and pour in some ice-cold water. Set the bowl of fish purée on the ice.

2   Lightly whip the cream until it just starts to thicken. Using a large metal spoon, gradually fold the cream into the fish, making sure each large dollop is smoothly incorporated before you add the next. Continue until the mixture is a soft mousse consistency which can hold its shape if piped. (You may not need to add all of the cream.) Chill.

3   Blanch the spinach in a pan of boiling water for about 30 seconds, or until just wilted. Drain, and refresh in a bowl of very cold water. Drain well again. Pick out only the whole leaves and lay them on kitchen paper towels to dry. Preheat the oven to 190°C/375°F/Gas Mark 5.

4   Lightly grease six ramekin dishes and line the bottom and sides with the spinach leaves, leaving some overhang all round. Spoon the mousse into a piping bag fitted with a large plain nozzle and pipe into the centre of each ramekin. Make sure the mousse covers the bottom. Tap the ramekin on the work surface until the mixture is level. Make a small hollow in the middle of each mousse using a teaspoon, and fill with the fish eggs. Smooth a little mousse on top to cover. Fold over the overhanging spinach leaves, then cover each ramekin with a disc of lightly oiled foil.

5   Stand the ramekins in a roasting tin and pour boiling water from a kettle around them to halfway up the sides, to form a bain-marie. Bake for about 15 minutes, or until the mousse feels just firm when lightly pressed. Remove from the bain-marie and allow to stand for 5 minutes before turning out on to warmed plates. Serve with a creamy velouté sauce or sauce américaine.

Serves 6

250g skinned fresh salmon fillet,
   any pin bones removed, then cut
   into chunks
1 tsp sea salt
freshly ground white pepper (optional)
2 tbsp fresh lemon juice
500–750ml double cream, chilled
about 300g whole spinach leaves,
   washed well and trimmed
about 50g salmon eggs or caviar
500ml Fish Velouté with Cream
   (page 62) or Sauce Américaine
   (page 68) to serve

Alternative fish: scallops
Recommended wines: Champagne
   or Soave Classico

It's very exciting – and economical – to make your own gravalax, especially when you are entertaining a large group. For a little fusion flair, I like to serve it with hot crispy beignets or fritters of fresh oysters in a fluffy tempura batter and a salad dressed with a honey and mustard vinaigrette.

gravalax with oysters in tempura batter

1   Skin the salmon above the blood line without removing the brown flesh next to the skin. Lay the fillet in a long, narrow dish. (You may need to cut it in half widthways to fit.)
2   Mix together the salt flakes, sugar and pepper. Finely chop the dill stalks and about one-third of the leaves and mix with the seasoning. Finely chop the rest of the dill leaves and reserve. Press half of the seasoning mixture evenly on to the fish, then turn over and repeat with the remainder. Cover with cling film. Place an oval plate on top and weigh down. Take care not to crush the fillet. Chill in the fridge for 24 hours.
3   Drain off the liquid from the dish. Rinse off the seasoned coating with cold water and pat dry with kitchen paper towels. Sprinkle the reserved chopped dill evenly on both sides of the salmon. Wrap tightly in cling film and chill for at least 3 more hours.
4   Using a long knife with a sharp, fine blade, cut wafer-thin slices from the fish, cutting lengthways at a slant starting from the tail end. Lay the slices on a clean tray.
5   To prepare the oysters, sift the flour into a small bowl. Gradually beat in the egg yolk and 150ml cold water until you have a smooth batter. Whisk the egg whites in a clean mixing bowl until firm, white and glossy. Using a large metal spoon, gently fold the whites into the batter, making sure they are evenly incorporated.
6   Mix the 3 tablespoons of flour with ½ teaspoon of salt. Toss the oysters into this coating mixture one by one, shaking off any excess.
7   Mix the vinaigrette with the mustard and honey and toss with the salad leaves. Make mounds of the dressed salad in the centre of each of six serving plates. Surround the salad with slices of gravalax, leaving gaps for the oysters, when ready.
8   Pour 2cm of oil into a deep frying pan and heat to 180°C/350°F, or until a cube of white bread turns brown in about 30 seconds. Dip each oyster into the foamy part of the batter, then gently drop into the oil. Fry for about 1 minute until the coating turns just golden brown. Keep whisking the batter as necessary so that it remains light and foamy for frying. As the oysters are fried, drain on kitchen paper towels. Arrange 3–4 oysters on each plate between the slices of gravalax and serve straight away.

Serves 6

1 side fresh salmon (whole fillet), about 1kg

75g sea salt flakes or rock salt

25g caster sugar

2 tbsp coarsely ground black pepper (or Aromatic Pepper Mix, page 40)

75g fresh dill

3 tbsp Classic Vinaigrette (page 76)

1 tsp coarse-grained mustard

1 tsp clear honey

300g mixed salad leaves

For the oysters:

80g self-raising flour + 3 tbsp for dusting

1 small egg yolk

2 egg whites

18–24 fresh rock oysters, shelled and cleaned

olive, groundnut or sunflower oil for frying

sea salt

Recommended wines: Muscadet or South African Sauvignon Blanc

salads

In this variation of the famous salad we use a homemade garlic, anchovy and lemon mayonnaise to dress Little Gem or baby Cos leaves, then serve with shavings of Parmesan and garlic croûtons.

caesar salad

Serves 4

juice ½ lemon

150ml Mustard Mayonnaise (page 66)

6 cloves garlic

12 anchovy fillets in oil, well drained
   and finely chopped

2 tbsp double cream

50g piece + 1 tbsp freshly grated
   Parmesan cheese

5 thick slices white bread,
   crusts removed

about 4 tbsp olive oil

4–6 Little Gem or baby Cos
   lettuces, chilled

freshly ground black pepper

Recommended wine: Chablis

1   Gradually mix the lemon juice into the mayonnaise, tasting as you go, using only as much as you wish. Crush 3 of the garlic cloves and beat into the mayonnaise together with the chopped anchovies, cream and the tablespoon of grated Parmesan cheese. The mayonnaise should be runny enough to coat the lettuce. If it seems too thick, beat in a few drops of water. Set aside.

2   Cut the other 3 cloves of garlic in half. Rub them over the bread slices, then cut the bread into 1cm cubes. In a frying pan, gently heat the olive oil with the halved garlic cloves just long enough to extract some flavour, then discard the garlic. Increase the heat of the oil and stir-fry the bread cubes until light golden brown all over. Take care not to burn the bread. Remove and drain on kitchen paper towels. Alternatively, you can crisp the croûtons in the oven (see below).

3   Separate the lettuces into single leaves and toss in half the mayonnaise dressing. Season with black pepper to taste.

4   Swirl the remaining dressing around the lettuce and scatter the croûtons over. Make Parmesan shavings from the block of cheese using a swivel vegetable peeler. Scatter around the shavings and serve immediately.

Variation

Making croûtons in the oven is easier than frying them. There is also less chance of them burning. Heat the oven to 170°C/325°F/Gas Mark 3. Toss the bread cubes in the garlic-flavoured oil in a bowl, or shake them together in a polythene bag, until thoroughly coated. Spread the cubes of bread out on a baking tray. Bake for about 20 minutes, or until light golden brown. Leave to cool and crisp up.

My former sous-chef Marcus Wareing, now at Pétrus in St James's, London, discovered this recipe while working in New York. There he learned how to utilize every part of a precious blue fin tuna. In his recipe, a large loin fillet is divided into four neat triangular fillets (a quarter of a 4–5kg loin is best for this). First, the fillets are marinated overnight in a simple mixture of coarse sea salt and lemon. The next day they are rolled in crushed peppercorns, then served wafer thin, carpaccio style, with a salad of mooli.

marinated tuna with balsamic-dressed mooli

Serves 6

long, thin tuna loin fillet, about 800g,
   preferably blue fin

100g coarse sea salt

grated zest and juice 1 lemon

2 tbsp coarsely crushed peppercorns
   (or one of my special mixes, page 40)

1 small shallot, finely chopped

2 tsp balsamic vinegar

2 tsp sesame oil

1 whole mooli (white radish), very finely
   sliced, preferably using a mandolin

100g mixed salad leaves

3 tbsp Classic Vinaigrette (page 76)

1 tbsp dark soy sauce

sea salt and freshly ground black pepper

Recommended wine: Santenay
   premier cru, Côte de Beaune

1   The day before serving, trim and neaten the tuna fillet into a long, even shape. Mix together the sea salt and lemon zest and juice and spread evenly over the fish. Roll very tightly into a long sausage shape in cling film. Place in the coldest part of the fridge and leave to marinate for 12 hours. Unwrap and rinse well in cold water. Pat dry with kitchen paper towels, then roll in the crushed peppercorns or special mix. Wrap well again and chill for another 12 hours.

2   The following day, about 3 hours before serving, prepare the dressing. In a small saucepan heat the shallot, vinegar and sesame oil until bubbling. Remove from the heat and leave to stand for about 1 hour. Mix the finely sliced mooli into the shallot dressing and leave to marinate for about 2 hours. At the same time, chill the tuna in the freezer for 2 hours.

3   To serve, unwrap the fish and slice into very fine discs. Spread the discs out on a tray. Season the salad leaves. Mix the vinaigrette with the soy sauce and toss one-third of this dressing with the salad. Arrange the salad in the centre of six dinner plates. Lay the mooli slices around the salad, then arrange the discs of tuna around the edge of the plates. Trickle over the remaining vinaigrette and serve.

Seafood and avocado make great partners, not least because of their contrasting textures and colour, complementing each other perfectly. Tians – little cakes – of crab salad topped with homemade guacamole and served with a chilli dressing make an elegant and succulent starter.

baby tians of crab and avocado

1   Flake the crab meat with a fork, removing any stray pieces of shell or cartilage as you go. Cut 2 of the tomatoes into quarters and de-seed. Using a fork, crush to a chunky purée. Mix the crab meat with the crushed tomato, the mayonnaise and a drop or two of Tabasco to taste. Season and set aside. Cut the remaining tomatoes into small petals or wedges, de-seed and set aside.

2   Now make the guacamole: peel 2 of the avocados and remove the stones, then mash the flesh to a chunky purée with a fork. Mix in the lime juice, spring onion, coriander or parsley and cumin. Season to taste. Divide into four. Set a round 8–10cm cutter in the centre of a serving plate and press in one-quarter of the guacamole. Spoon one-quarter of the crab meat on top, then lift off the cutter. Repeat on three more serving plates.

3   Peel and stone the remaining avocado. Slice neatly and brush with a little of the vinaigrette to prevent it browning. Arrange the slices around the tians along with the tomato wedges or petals. Whisk the remaining vinaigrette with the chilli spice mix. Trickle over the avocado and tomato garnish. Serve immediately.

Serves 4

200g white crab meat

4 ripe plum tomatoes, skinned

2 tbsp Mustard Mayonnaise (page 66)

few drops Tabasco sauce

3 ripe avocados

2 tsp fresh lime juice

1 small spring onion, finely chopped

1 tbsp chopped fresh coriander
   or parsley

good pinch ground cumin

4 tbsp Classic Vinaigrette (page 76)

1 tsp Chilli Spice Mix (page 74)

sea salt and freshly ground black pepper

Recommended wine: Touraine
   Sauvignon Blanc

Tender baby squid need the lightest of cooking. I like to fill them with this Mediterranean mixture of couscous and finely chopped ratatouille vegetables, then grill them just before serving with a piquant sauce and a little salad. A heavy-based, ridged grill pan is ideal for cooking the squid.

baby squid with couscous ratatouille

1   First prepare the filling: in a bowl, cover the couscous with 300ml of boiling water. Stir in 1 teaspoon of salt and 1 tablespoon of the olive oil. Leave to soak for 1 hour, stirring occasionally with a fork to break down the lumps of grains. It may help to rub the grains with your fingers.

2   Purée the tomato in a food processor or blender, or crush with a fork. Mix into the soaked couscous.

3   Heat 2 tablespoons of the remaining oil in a saucepan and gently sauté the peppers, aubergine and courgette for about 7 minutes, or until softened. Season, then mix into the couscous. Heat another tablespoon of oil in a small sauté pan and stir-fry the squid tentacles for 1–2 minutes until just cooked. Take care not to overcook. Drain, season and allow to cool.

4   Wash the squid tubes well and pat dry with kitchen paper towels. Fill with the couscous mixture, pressing it in firmly with the back of a teaspoon. Secure the tops with wooden cocktail sticks. Toss the stuffed squid with the last tablespoon of oil and lightly season with salt and pepper.

5   Heat a ridged grill pan or top-heat grill until hot. Cook the squid for 3–5 minutes, or until the flesh just turns white and feels firm. Turn the squid once or twice, taking care not to overcook or they will become tough. Remove from the heat and allow to stand for 5 minutes before removing the sticks.

6   Meanwhile, toss the salad leaves with the sautéed tentacles. Season well and mix with the vinaigrette. Arrange the salad in the middle of each of four serving plates. Arrange four or five squid over the salad and trickle over the sauce vierge. Garnish with basil leaves and chives. Serve immediately.

Serves 4

150g couscous

5 tbsp olive oil

1 large tomato, skinned and de-seeded

½ red pepper, finely diced

½ yellow pepper, finely diced

½ small aubergine, finely diced

1 small courgette, finely diced

16–20 baby squid, each about 5cm
   diameter, prepared

100g mixed salad leaves

1 tbsp Classic Vinaigrette (page 76)

150ml Sauce Vierge (page 69)

4 sprigs fresh basil

a few fresh chives

sea salt and freshly ground black pepper

Recommended wine: an Oregon
   Pinot Noir

Here, lightly grilled sardines and guacamole are topped with fresh pesto and served with dressed salad leaves. Fresh sardines never fail to evoke sunny weather and Mediterranean beach food for me. They are now easy to come by. Ask your fishmonger to fillet them for you, or follow the instructions on page 28.

marinated sardines with avocado and pesto

Serves 4

8 large fresh sardines, filleted
  and with skin on
4 tsp olive oil
tips from 2 sprigs fresh thyme
1 tbsp fresh lemon juice
2 ripe avocados
2 tsp fresh lime juice
1 small spring onion, finely chopped
1 tbsp chopped fresh parsley
good pinch ground cumin
2 tbsp Classic Vinaigrette (page 76)
200g mixed salad leaves
150ml Fresh Pesto (page 75)
sea salt and freshly ground black pepper

Recommended wine: Gavi di Gavi

1   Remove any pin bones from the sardine fillets with your fingernails or tweezers, if necessary. Mix together the oil, thyme and lemon juice in a shallow dish and add the fillets, turning to coat. Cover and set aside to marinate for about 20 minutes.

2   Meanwhile, make the guacamole. Halve the avocados, remove the stones and peel. Place the flesh in a bowl and mash to a chunky purée with a fork. Mix in the lime juice, spring onion, parsley and cumin. Season and set aside.

4   Preheat the grill to hot, then cook the fillets, skin side up, for 3–5 minutes, or until the skin is crisp and the flesh just firm when pressed. There is no need to turn the fish. Remove from the grill, season and set aside.

5   Toss 1 tablespoon of the vinaigrette with the salad leaves and season. Mix the remaining vinaigrette into the pesto and add a drop or two of water to make a running consistency.

6   Now assemble the salad: spoon the guacamole into the centre of four plates, or shape it using a round plain cutter. Arrange the dressed salad on top. Drizzle the pesto sauce around the avocado and salad. Cut each sardine fillet in half and place four halves on each plate on top of the pesto. Serve at once.

This eye-catching salad allows you to vary the ingredients to suit your taste. For example, you may prefer to use warm-water tiger prawns or the fuller-flavoured langoustines. I like to add finely chopped black truffle to the dressing, but you could add a few drops of truffle olive oil instead, for a similar flavour. Alternatively, a teaspoon of coarse-grained mustard gives a different, yet equally delicious, flavour.

prawn and artichoke salad with truffle dressing

1   Remove all the leaves from the artichokes. Cut out the hairy chokes and slice off the stalk, leaving the hearts only. Cut these into thin slices. Add the lemon juice to a bowl of cold water and submerge the artichoke slices in it to stop them browning.

2   Bring a saucepan of salted water to the boil and blanch the green beans for 2 minutes. Drain and refresh under cold water. Drain again and set aside.

3   Drain the artichoke slices and pat dry on kitchen paper towels. In a sauté pan, heat the groundnut oil and cook the artichokes for 3 minutes until softened. Add the beans and stir-fry until heated through. Drain on kitchen paper towels. Season and mix with half the chopped truffle or truffle oil.

4   Bring another pan of water to the boil and drop in the prawns or langoustines. Cook for 3 minutes, or until they turn pink and feel firm. Drain, and peel when cool enough to handle. Toss with 1 tablespoon of the vinaigrette and season.

5   Mix the lamb's lettuce with 2 tablespoons of the vinaigrette and season. Mix the remaining vinaigrette with the rest of the chopped truffle or truffle oil.

6   Place a mound of artichokes and beans in the centre of each plate. Top with the lamb's lettuce and arrange the prawns or langoustines around the leaves. Trickle the truffle dressing around the plate and over the prawns, then serve.

Serves 4

4 large globe artichokes

2 tbsp fresh lemon juice

200g whole green beans, cut into
   2cm lengths

2 tbsp groundnut oil

1 tsp finely chopped black truffle or
   a few dashes truffle olive oil

20 raw tiger prawns or langoustines

6 tbsp Classic Vinaigrette (page 76)

200g lamb's lettuce (mâche)

sea salt and freshly ground black pepper

Alternative fish: cold-water prawns

Recommended wine: white
   Crozes-Hermitage

Found in the tropics, snappers have the most beautiful pink hues and their rich, meaty flesh is perfect for grilling. Mixed with Western globe artichokes and potatoes, then finished with a spicy French dressing, this recipe is an example of what is now referred to as fusion food – blending ingredients from all over the world into a harmonious and enticing whole.

oriental snapper salad

Serves 4

1 large snapper, about 1kg, filleted
  into 4 with skin on

4 medium globe artichokes

2 tbsp fresh lemon juice

400g new potatoes

2–3 tsp sesame oil

2 tbsp olive oil

100ml Classic Vinaigrette (page 76)
  + extra for serving

1 tsp Chilli Spice Mix (page 74)

300g mixed salad leaves, ideally with
  frilly leaves

sea salt and freshly ground black pepper

Alternative fish: bream, large mackerel,
  swordfish steaks

Recommended wine: Beaujolais-
  Villages

1   Check the fish for pin bones and remove any you find with your fingernails or tweezers. Season and set aside.

2   Remove all the leaves from the artichokes. Cut out the hairy chokes and slice off the stalk, leaving the hearts only. Cut these into thick slices. Add the lemon juice to a bowl of cold water and submerge the artichoke slices in it to stop them browning.

3   Boil the new potatoes and drain. Peel off their skins, then slice. Wearing rubber gloves makes the hot potatoes easier to handle.

4   Drain the artichoke slices and pat dry on kitchen paper towels. In a large non-stick frying pan, heat the sesame oil with 1 tablespoon of the olive oil. Fry the artichokes for 5 minutes, or until a light golden brown colour and slightly tender. Add the potato slices to the pan and cook for another 5 minutes until light gold. Season to taste.

5   Meanwhile, in another large non-stick frying pan, heat the remaining olive oil and add the snapper fillets, skin side first. Cook for about 5 minutes in all, or until the skin is crisp and coloured and the flesh feels just firm. Remove from the pan and drain on kitchen paper towels.

6   Stir half the vinaigrette into the chilli spice mix to make a dressing and set aside. Dress the salad with the remaining vinaigrette. Make a dainty mound of salad at the top of each serving plate. Arrange the artichokes and potatoes in the centre of each plate. Place the snapper fillets on top of the vegetables. Lightly coat the fish with the chilli vinaigrette, then serve straight away.

A warm salad made in the southern-French style: pretty pan-fried red mullet fillets on a creamy purée of aubergine, surrounded by a light tomato dressing. This dish makes a great start to any meal.

red mullet salad with aubergine caviar and tomato vinaigrette

Serves 4

1 medium aubergine

1 large clove garlic, crushed

rock or sea salt

1 sprig fresh rosemary

8 x 100g red mullet fillets, skin on

1 tbsp olive oil

250g mixed salad leaves

1–2 tbsp Classic Vinaigrette (page 76)

freshly ground black pepper

For the dressing:

3 ripe plum tomatoes, skinned and
   de-seeded

100ml olive oil

juice ½ lemon

1 tsp chopped fresh basil

1 tsp chopped fresh tarragon

½ tsp balsamic vinegar

Alternative fish: mackerel, monkfish

Recommended wine: a Provençal rosé

1   Preheat the oven to 220°C/425°F/Gas Mark 7. Cut the aubergine in half lengthways and score the flesh. Smear the crushed garlic on the cut surface of both halves and season with rock or sea salt. Sandwich the sprig of rosemary between the two halves and press them together. Wrap tightly in foil and bake for 45 minutes, then reduce the heat to 110°C/225°F/Gas Mark Low. Bake for a further 25 minutes, or until the skins have shrivelled and the flesh is squashy.

2   Carefully unwrap the aubergine and save any juices in a bowl. Discard the rosemary, then scrape the flesh and garlic into the same bowl, discarding the skin. Chop the flesh well until pulpy, then transfer to a saucepan. Cook over a medium heat, stirring occasionally, for about 5 minutes until reduced down and thickened. Season to taste, then set this aubergine caviar aside.

3   To make the dressing, chop the tomatoes into very fine dice, almost a purée, but not too runny. Scoop into a bowl and mix in the oil, lemon juice, basil, tarragon and vinegar. Season and set aside.

4   Remove any pin bones from the fish. In a large non-stick pan, heat the oil and fry the fillets, skin side down, for 3 minutes. Carefully flip them over and cook the other side for 2 minutes. Remove and season. Cut each fillet into two lengthways.

5   Dress the salad leaves with the vinaigrette and season. Arrange the salad in the centre of four large plates. Make four small mounds of aubergine caviar on each plate around the salad and top each mound with a fillet half. Swirl the tomato dressing around the fish and serve immediately.

Smoked trout has a succulent, delicate flavour. Here it is teamed with an unusual aubergine salsa and an anchovy-dressed salad, and garnished with halved quail's eggs. Serve with thinly sliced rye bread.

smoked trout with spicy aubergine salsa and anchovy-dressed leaves

1   First, make the aubergine salsa. Heat 2 tablespoons of the oil in a saucepan and gently cook the aubergine and shallots, stirring occasionally, for about 10 minutes or until they are soft.

2   Add the vinegar, spices and gherkins and cook for a further 2 minutes. Season lightly, then remove from the heat. Stir in the remaining oil and set aside to cool. When tepid, stir in the chopped fresh herbs. Remove the cardamom pods.

3   Meanwhile, skin the trout, remove the head and ease the flesh off the main bones with the back of a thin-bladed knife. You should end up with 4 long, neat fillets from each fish.

4   Peel the eggs, rinse in cold water and halve. Quail's eggs have quite tough little shells and are best peeled in small sections. This is easier if you first roll the eggs in their shells until the shell cracks.

5   To make the dressing, pat the anchovy fillets dry on kitchen paper towels. Place in a food processor together with all the other ingredients and whizz until smooth and creamy, scraping down the sides of the container once or twice. The dressing should be sufficiently runny to coat the salad. If necessary, add up to 2 teaspoons of cold water in careful dribbles until it is the correct consistency.

6   Arrange the trout fillets in the centre of four plates and spoon the salsa around in a circle. Toss the salad leaves with the dressing and pile neatly on top of the fillets. Arrange 3 egg halves on the salad for each plate and top them with a sprig of parsley.

Serves 4

4 x 300g whole smoked trout

6 quail's eggs, hard-boiled

about 200g mixed salad leaves

4 small sprigs fresh flat-leaf parsley

For the aubergine salsa:

3 tbsp olive oil

1 large aubergine, finely diced

3 large shallots, finely chopped

2 tsp sherry vinegar

1 tsp each ground cumin and garam masala

6 whole cardamoms

2 gherkins, finely diced

1 tbsp each chopped fresh coriander,
   basil and chives

sea salt and freshly ground black pepper

For the anchovy dressing:

50g can anchovy fillets, drained

150ml olive oil

1 tbsp white wine vinegar

1 small garlic clove, peeled and crushed

Recommended wine: Chilean
   Chardonnay

And now for something completely different ... pan-roasted scallops served as a warm salad with a unique dressing I learnt in New York – simply a purée of sultanas (white raisins) and capers. This dressing works well with other pan-fried fish too. For a glamorous and more elaborate presentation, set each scallop half on a little dab of cauliflower purée (page 210). I also like to garnish the plates with tiny fritters of cauliflower florets.

salad of pan-roasted scallops with white raisin and caper dressing

1   Put the sultanas, capers and 120ml of water in a food processor. Season, then blend until very smooth, scraping down the sides of the container once or twice. Pass through a sieve, rubbing with the back of a ladle or a wooden spoon. The dressing should have a pouring consistency. If it seems too thick, add a little extra water. Set aside.

2   Lightly sprinkle pinches of the curry powder on both sides of the scallops. Heat the oil in a large non-stick frying pan. Add the scallops, placing them clockwise in the pan. Cook for just 1 minute on each side, turning them in the same order as they were placed. (This ensures that they each cook for the same amount of time.) When nicely brown on each side and bouncy when pressed, remove from the pan. Cool for a minute or two, then slice each in half horizontally. Season well.

3   Dress the salad leaves with the vinaigrette and divide among four plates. Place 6 or 7 scallop halves per plate around the salad. Drizzle the raisin dressing over the scallops, or spoon it between them in little mounds if you prefer, and serve straight away while still warm.

Serves 4

100g sultanas (white raisins)

100g drained capers

about 1 tsp mild curry powder

12–14 large scallops, shelled, trimmed
  and cleaned

1 tbsp olive oil

200g mixed salad leaves

2 tbsp Classic Vinaigrette (page 76)

sea salt and freshly ground black pepper

Recommended wine: Grüner Veltliner
  Spätlese Trocken, Austria

risottos and pasta

Once you have mastered the technique of getting the creamy texture of the rice just right while retaining a good al dente bite, it's just a matter of adding the other ingredients to make the perfect risotto.

basic risotto

Serves 4

500–600ml Fish Stock (pages 58–59) or
   Chicken Stock (page 61) or
   Vegetable Nage (page 61)

3 tbsp olive oil

2 large shallots, finely chopped

200g risotto rice (Carnaroli, Arborio or
   Vialone Nano)

100ml dry white wine

Flavourings of your choice
   (pages 127–130)

2 tbsp mascarpone cheese

1–2 tbsp freshly grated Parmesan
   cheese (optional)

sea salt and freshly ground black pepper

Use a 'super fini' quality of risotto rice – Carnaroli, Arborio or the more 'wholegrain' Vialone Nano. These give a starchy creaminess to the dish without breaking down.

Prepare all the other ingredients in advance before you begin to cook the rice, so that you can add them as soon as you have finished making the basic risotto.

Lightly toast the grains of rice in the pan before adding the stock or wine. The pan should hiss gratefully as the liquid is poured in.

Add the stock one ladleful at a time, with each amount stirred in and absorbed before the next is added. Keep the stock at a gentle simmer as you ladle it in.

Par-cook the risotto for about 12 minutes, then cool and chill it before finishing it off just before serving, with the rest of the stock and your chosen flavourings.

1   Pour the stock into a saucepan and heat to a gentle simmer.

2   In a medium saucepan, heat the oil and gently sauté the shallots for 5 minutes, or until softened and lightly coloured. Add the rice and cook over a medium to high heat for 2–3 minutes, stirring frequently. Pour in the wine and stir until it has been absorbed. Ladle in one-quarter of the stock and cook, stirring frequently, over a medium heat until the liquid is almost completely absorbed.

3   Add another ladleful of stock and stir again until absorbed. Continue in this way until the rice has been cooking for about 12 minutes. You should have some stock left over. If eating straight away, go to step 5.

4   If cooking the risotto ahead of time, stop cooking at this point and drain the risotto mixture in a sieve set over a bowl. Mix the liquid in the bowl with the remaining stock. Spread the par-cooked risotto out on a baking tray to cool. (This stops the cooking.)

5   Continue cooking, gradually adding the remaining stock, until the grains of rice are plump and creamy. The total cooking time should be about 15–18 minutes, and the amount of stock you use will vary. If you run out of stock, you can add boiling water.

6   Add your chosen flavouring plus the mascarpone and Parmesan, if using. Season to taste, stir well and serve.

Use hot-smoked eels for this – that is, ones that have been cooked and smoked. Check carefully for any bones before cutting up the eels.

risotto with smoked eel and baby onions

1   Fold the diced eel into the risotto halfway through the cooking time (at the end of step 4, opposite).

2   While you finish cooking the risotto, heat the butter and oil in a saucepan. Sauté the onions over a medium heat for about 5 minutes, or until they start to turn golden brown. Add about one-quarter of the stock and cook until reduced right down, then add the rest. Cover and simmer for a further 5 minutes, or until the onions are quite soft. Increase the heat and cook, uncovered, until all the liquid has evaporated and the onions are nicely glazed. Stir into the cooked risotto and serve immediately.

Serves 4

500g smoked eel, skinned if necessary, boned and finely diced

Basic Risotto (opposite)

75g butter

2 tbsp olive oil

about 200g baby onions, peeled

250ml Fish Stock (pages 58–59), Chicken Stock (page 61) or Vegetable Nage (page 61)

Alternative fish: hot-smoked salmon, flaked

Recommended wine: white Graves

Tender rings and tentacles of squid, lightly pan-roasted and flavoured with their cooking juices, are quick to prepare and make a succulent addition to a creamy risotto.

risotto with pan-roasted squid

1   Slice the squid tubes into 1cm thick rings and pat dry with kitchen paper towels.

2   In a sauté pan, heat the oil and quickly stir-fry the squid rings and tentacles for two to three minutes, or until just firm and white. Take care not to overcook. Remove with a slotted spoon.

3   Stir the shallot into the oil and gently sauté for about 5 minutes, or until softened. Add the vinegar and cook until reduced by half. Whisk in the butter until it melts and the sauce is glossy.

4   Return the squid to the pan and lightly season. Fold into the risotto just as you finish making it. Garnish with the chervil and serve immediately.

Serves 4

4 baby or 2 medium squid, prepared

1 tbsp olive oil

1 large shallot, finely chopped

90ml balsamic vinegar

2 tsp butter

Basic Risotto (page 126)

sprigs fresh chervil to garnish

sea salt and freshly ground
    black pepper

Recommended wines: Baron de 'L',
    Ladoucette, Château du Nozet

A risotto with a touch of class. If morel mushrooms are tricky to find, you could use dried ones, soaked to rehydrate, or any other interesting wild mushrooms you may find in the shops or, even better, in the woods.

risotto with lobster and morels

Serves 4

1 small cooked lobster

2 tbsp olive oil

1 large shallot, finely chopped

12 fresh morels, halved, or 6 dried
   morels, soaked and quartered

Basic Risotto (page 126)

Sea salt and freshly ground
   black pepper

Recommended wine: Meursault
   premier cru

1   Remove the tail meat from the lobster in one piece, then cut across into slices. Crack open the claws, extract the meat using a skewer and cut into fine dice.

2   In a frying pan, heat 1 tablespoon of the oil and sauté the shallot for 5 minutes, or until softened. Stir in the morels and cook for 2 minutes. Add the diced lobster claw meat and cook until just reheated. Remove from the pan and keep warm.

3   Heat the remaining oil and lightly sauté the sliced lobster tail meat for about 3 minutes to reheat and give a caramelized flavour.

4   Gently fold the mixture of shallot, mushrooms and diced lobster into the risotto just as you finish making it. Season to taste. Garnish with the sliced lobster and serve.

I love the feel of the fresh pasta sheets as they pass through the rollers and emerge thinner with every turn. For quick dishes you will find bought fresh or quality dried pasta is acceptable, but for special dishes such as ravioli, sheets of homemade pasta are easier to handle. The recipe here makes enough pasta for about 12 servings. Any pasta that you don't want to use right away can be cut into tagliatelle or spaghetti, curled into 'nests' and then frozen until you need it. When you do, simply drop the frozen nests into boiling water and cook for just 2 minutes, then drain and use straight away.

basic pasta dough

Makes about 900g

550g plain flour or soft-wheat Italian
  pasta flour

½ tsp fine sea salt

4 large free-range eggs

6 egg yolks

2 tbsp olive oil

1   Sift the flour and salt into a bowl. Tip into a food processor with the eggs, yolks and oil. Blend until you have fine crumbs, stopping the machine occasionally and scraping down the sides of the container. Continue to process until the mixture just starts to form small lumps. You can check this by pressing a small amount between your thumb and finger. When it forms a smooth, firm paste, it is ready.

2   Transfer the mixture to a very lightly floured surface. With the palm of your hand, knead it into a smooth ball, firmly but not too vigorously, for 3–5 minutes. The dough should feel smooth and slightly springy. Wrap in cling film and set aside for 1–2 hours.

3   To roll the pasta dough, set the rollers on the pasta machine to the thickest setting. Break off a piece of dough the size of a large egg. Lightly flour the dough, then feed it through the rollers 3 or 4 times. Click the setting to the next number and feed the dough through again 3 or 4 times. As you roll, gently support the underside of the dough with the back of your hand.

4   Continue in this way until you reach the finest setting. By now the sheet of dough should be smooth, thin and straight. If you intend to put it through cutters, you may need to dust it with a little flour to stop it sticking. Alternatively, you can hang it over the back of a chair to dry out for half an hour or so. However, make sure the dough does not become too dry or it will crack. Here are the appropriate widths for the following types of pasta: spaghetti (rolled thicker for a rounder shape) – 5mm; tagliatelle – 1cm; pappardelle – about 3cm; sheets for lasagne, cannelloni and ravioli – the width depends on the size of your pasta machine.

5   Cook fresh pasta strips in salted boiling water for 1–2 minutes, then drain and toss with a little butter. Do not overdrain as fresh pasta is always best served slightly wet.

When fresh clams are in season and readily available, this sauce is well worth making as an accompaniment for homemade pasta. Clams are prepared very simply by washing in a bowl under plenty of cold running water. They do not have 'beards' like mussels.

spaghetti with clams and tarragon

1   Fill a large bowl with cold water, then tip in the clams. Swish them round with your hand. Leave the cold tap running gently into the bowl for about 10 minutes, until the clams are thoroughly clean. Drain and discard any with opened shells.

2   Put the clams in a large pan. Add the sliced shallot, tarragon stalks and wine. Bring to the boil, then cover tightly with the lid and simmer for about 5 minutes. Drain the clams, reserving the cooking liquid in another pan. Discard any unopened clams and set the rest aside.

3   Add the chopped shallot and lemon juice to the pan of cooking liquid. Boil until reduced by half. Whisk in the butter, then stir in the tomato concassé and the tarragon leaves.

4   Cook the spaghetti in plenty of salted boiling water for a minute or two. Drain and mix it gently with the sauce and cooked clams. Season to taste. Garnish with tarragon and serve.

Serves 4

1kg fresh clams

2 large shallots, 1 thinly sliced, 1 finely chopped

2 large sprigs fresh tarragon, stalks reserved and leaves cut in strips + extra to garnish

300ml dry white wine

1 tbsp fresh lemon juice

15g butter

2 ripe plum tomatoes, concassé (page 218)

300g fresh spaghetti (opposite)

sea salt and freshly ground black pepper

Alternative fish: mussels

Recommended wine: Penedés Sauvignon Blanc

Smoked salmon and pasta make excellent companions for a quick and simple supper dish. But please, no Parmesan sprinkled on top – the flavours of the fish and pasta are too subtle.

pappardelle with smoked salmon and sauce vierge

1   Make up the sauce vierge, set aside and keep warm. Cook the fresh pasta for just a minute or two in plenty of salted boiling water, then drain and toss with a little butter.

2   Fold the salmon strips into the cooked pasta. Season to taste. Serve on to plates and spoon over the sauce vierge.

Serves 3–4

150ml Sauce Vierge (page 69)

250–300g fresh pappardelle (page 132)

butter for pasta

200g smoked salmon, cut into
   thin strips

sea salt and freshly ground black pepper

Recommended wine: white Bordeaux

For this recipe you will need to make some fresh basil purée for the sauce, but you can also use it to flavour pasta dough by substituting 2 teaspoons of it for one of the eggs.

tagliatelle with basil sauce and tuna

Serves 4

250ml Vegetable Nage (page 61) or
   Fish Stock (pages 58–59)

100ml double cream

2 tsp fresh basil purée (page 75)

1 tbsp olive oil

4 x 120–150g fresh tuna steaks,
   preferably yellow fin for a lighter flavour

2 tbsp brandy

300g fresh tagliatelle (page 132)

1–2 tsp butter + extra for pasta

sea salt and freshly ground black pepper

Alternative fish: salmon, swordfish

Recommended wine: a light Spanish
   Grenache

1   Pour the nage or fish stock into a small saucepan. Bring to the boil and cook for about 10 minutes until reduced by half. Stir in the cream and the basil purée, then set this sauce aside.

2   Heat the oil in a large non-stick frying pan and fry the tuna for about 2–3 minutes on each side. The fish should be just cooked and still feel slightly springy. Season lightly. Add the brandy and set alight, then remove the pan from the heat.

3   Cook the tagliatelle for a minute or two in plenty of salted boiling water, then drain and toss with a little butter. Reheat the sauce, then whisk in 1–2 teaspoons butter. Fold into the pasta and serve immediately with the tuna steaks on top.

Possibly the ultimate simple main course – spaghetti cooked al dente in a light velouté sauce with caviar and crème fraîche. This is a good recipe to turn to when you've got a batch of frozen velouté sauce in the freezer to use up. For an even quicker version of this dish, drain the spaghetti, leaving it slightly wet, and toss with a little butter, then add the caviar and crème fraîche. Either of these methods is a good way of stretching a single serving of caviar to feed four.

spaghetti with caviar and crème fraîche

1   Gently reheat the fish velouté until almost boiling, then keep warm. If using fish stock, bring to the boil, then reduce until you have 100ml.

2   Cook the pasta in plenty of lightly salted boiling water for 2 minutes if using fresh spaghetti; follow the packet instructions if using dried pasta. Drain, leaving slightly wet.

3   Mix the crème fraîche into the velouté or stock. Stir in the chervil or parsley and the caviar. Take great care not to let the sauce overheat or boil as the caviar will harden and be wasted.

4   Toss the sauce with the pasta, season to taste and serve immediately. For a smart presentation, you may like to serve with one-quarter of the caviar placed on each serving of pasta, rather than mixed into the sauce.

Serves 4

100ml Fish Velouté with Cream
   (page 62) or 200ml Fish Stock
   (pages 58–59)
450g fresh spaghetti (page 132) or
   400g good-quality dried spaghetti
4 tbsp crème fraîche
2 tbsp chopped fresh chervil or parsley
20g caviar
sea salt and freshly ground black pepper

Alternative fish: salmon eggs (don't use
   lumpfish roe!)
Recommended wine: Alsace Riesling

This dish uses both the white and brown crab meat from two medium crabs, which you can buy ready-prepared from a fishmonger if you don't want to do the job yourself. As an alternative to the Sauce Vierge, you could serve a vinaigrette flavoured with a well-reduced lobster or crab stock.

crab ravioli with sauce vierge

Serves 4

300g white crab meat

a little fresh lemon juice to taste

150g brown crab meat, or peeled
  cold-water prawns, whizzed in
  a food processor to a purée

½ tsp chopped fresh basil

½ tsp chopped fresh tarragon

½ tsp chopped fresh chervil

200g fresh pasta dough (page 132),
  thinly rolled

150ml Sauce Vierge (page 69)

sprigs fresh chervil or flat-leaf parsley
  to garnish

sea salt and freshly ground black pepper

Recommended wine: Canadian
  Pinot Blanc

1   Make the filling first: finely flake the white crab meat, removing any pieces of shell or cartilage. Season well and mix in some lemon juice to taste and the chopped herbs. Use the brown crab meat or prawn purée to bind the mixture. (You may not need it all.)

2   With clean and very dry hands, shape the mixture into four balls. Chill the balls to firm up while you work with the pasta dough.

3   Lay the sheets of pasta dough on the work surface and cut out 8 rounds using a 10cm cutter. Lightly brush the edges of the pasta rounds with a little water. Place a crab ball in the centre of four of the rounds. Top with the remaining rounds and press the edges together to seal, using a thumb and forefinger, making sure that the dough is pressed against the filling with no air gaps. For a professional finish, you can press a fluted cutter, a size smaller than the plain cutter, around the filled raviolis to seal the edges firmly and cut a decorative edge.

4   Bring a saucepan of water to the boil, then cook the ravioli for 2 minutes. Remove with a slotted spoon. Drain and transfer to four warmed soup plates. Drizzle over the sauce, garnish with the chervil or parsley and serve.

Raw tiger prawns and fresh basil combine to make a flavoursome filling for homemade cannelloni. The addition of cream and a hollandaise sauce elevates this dish into something of a luxury.

cannelloni of prawns with tarragon hollandaise

Serves 2–4

300g raw tiger prawns, peeled

4 tbsp double cream

1 tsp chopped fresh basil

200g homemade pasta dough
  (page 132), thinly rolled

1 tbsp chopped fresh tarragon and a
  few sprigs to garnish

150ml Olive Oil Hollandaise (page 64)

2 tsp olive oil

sea salt and freshly ground black pepper

Alternative fish: cold-water Atlantic
  prawns

Recommended wine: Chilean
  Chardonnay

1   Pat the prawns dry with kitchen paper towels. Blend one-third of them in a food processor until smooth, scraping down the sides of the container once or twice. Add the cream and seasoning and blend again. Spoon into a bowl and stir in the basil. Finely chop half the remaining prawns and mix into the purée.

2   Cut the sheets of pasta dough into four 10 x 15cm strips. In a large pan of salted boiling water, blanch the strips for about 10 seconds. Drain and pat dry with kitchen paper towels. Place each strip on a piece of cling film. Spoon one-quarter of the prawn filling along a short end of each pasta strip. Roll up fairly tightly and wrap in the cling film, twisting the ends to seal. Chill for about 30 minutes.

3   Stir the chopped tarragon into the hollandaise sauce, then thin down a little with 2 tablespoons warm water. The sauce should be a coating consistency. Keep warm.

4   In a sauté pan, heat the oil and fry the remaining prawns until just pink. Set aside to use as a garnish. Preheat the grill.

5   Bring a large shallow pan of water to the boil. Blanch the cannelloni, in their cling-film wrappings, for 4 minutes. Drain. When cool enough to handle, carefully unwrap and arrange in a shallow heatproof dish. Coat with the sauce. Cook under the grill until bubbling and lightly browned. Garnish with the pan-fried prawns and sprigs of tarragon, then serve immediately.

Mine is a rather luxurious version of this popular family dish. The recipe uses a velouté sauce, preferably the version with cream but, if you are in a hurry, the flour-based version is fine. For the pasta, try to use fresh or homemade pasta sheets, although good-quality dried lasagne could be substituted. Avoid using the 'no-cook' lasagne sheets, as they tend to be gummy.

smoked haddock lasagne with mustard sauce

1   Pour the milk or water into a large saucepan or deep frying pan and bring to a simmer. Submerge the haddock in the liquid, adding more milk or water if necessary to cover. Poach for about 5 minutes, or until the flesh just starts to flake, then drain. Skin, bone and flake the fish while still hot and set the flesh aside.

2   Blanch the lasagne sheets in a saucepan of salted boiling water: just 2 minutes for fresh sheets and 4–5 minutes for dried. Drain and rinse in cold water, then pat dry with kitchen paper towels. Set aside.

3   In a frying pan, heat the oil and sauté the mushrooms until just softened. Remove and drain. Blanch the asparagus for 2 minutes in boiling water, then drain.

4   Reheat the velouté sauce. Stir in the mustard and chives and check the seasoning. Keep the sauce warm.

5   To assemble the lasagne: preheat the oven to 190°C/375°F/Gas Mark 5. Lightly grease a medium-sized ovenproof dish. Pour a little sauce on the bottom of the dish and arrange a layer of the pasta sheets on top (about one-third). Scatter over one-third of the spinach leaves. Arrange one-third of the fish on top, then add one-third of the mushrooms. Trickle over a little more sauce. Repeat the layers twice more, then arrange the blanched asparagus on top. Pour over the last of the sauce and sprinkle with the Parmesan cheese. Bake for about 15 minutes, or until hot and bubbling. Allow to stand for about 10 minutes before serving.

Serves 4

about 500ml skimmed milk or water

1 large Finnan haddock, about 1kg

300g fresh lasagne sheets (page 132)
   or 150g dried lasagne

2 tbsp olive oil

200g wild or cultivated mushrooms
   of your choice, sliced

12–16 asparagus tips, stalks peeled

500ml Fish Velouté (page 62)

1 tbsp coarse-grained mustard

1 tbsp chopped fresh chives

150g baby spinach leaves, well-washed

1 tbsp freshly grated Parmesan cheese

sea salt and freshly ground black pepper

Alternative fish: other smoked fish
   of your choice

Recommended wine: Bourgogne
   Rouge

homestyle fish

A very easy dish. Just spend a little time on the initial preparation and you'll find the cooking takes only minutes. You'll need a good sized, non-stick or well-seasoned wok for this. Pak choi (also called bok choy) is a Chinese leafy vegetable, rather like Swiss chard. It is increasingly available in supermarkets but, if you can't find it, then use shredded Chinese leaves instead. Serve with a bowl of aromatic Thai jasmine rice sprinkled with a few toasted sesame seeds.

stir-fried monkfish with peppers and pak choi

1   Remove any grey membrane from the monkfish, then cut across into 1cm slices. Make sure all the other ingredients are prepared before you start cooking.

2   Heat a large wok until almost smoking. Add 1 tablespoon of the oil and stir-fry the monkfish for about 3 minutes, until browned on both sides. Remove and drain on kitchen paper towels. Keep hot.

3   Add the remaining oil to the wok and heat well. Stir-fry the peppers, onion, ginger and courgette for about 2 minutes, until cooked and lightly coloured. Remove from the wok with a draining spoon and keep warm.

4   Reheat the oil and stir-fry the pak choi and bean sprouts for 2 minutes, or until just wilted. Mix in the soy sauce and 1 teaspoon of the spice mix. Mix the remaining ½ teaspoon of spice mix into the vinaigrette. Set aside.

5   Return the other vegetables to the wok. Toss in the sesame oil and reheat until very hot. Check the seasoning. Divide among four warmed plates and arrange the monkfish on top. Trickle a little of the spicy vinaigrette on top of each portion, then serve.

Serves 4

2 x 250g monkfish tails, filleted

2 tbsp groundnut oil

1 small red pepper, thinly sliced

1 small yellow pepper, thinly sliced

1 small onion, thinly sliced

1 tbsp chopped fresh ginger

1 medium courgette, sliced

about 100g pak choi, coarsely shredded

50g fresh bean sprouts

2 tsp light soy sauce

1½ tsp Chilli Spice Mix (page 74)

2 tbsp Classic Vinaigrette (page 76)

1 tsp sesame oil

sea salt and freshly ground black pepper

Alternative fish: peeled tiger prawns, about 400g

Recommended wine: Australian Chardonnay

This dish brings back memories of sunny meals in the Mediterranean where small, tender monkfish tails are roasted in Italian pancetta. Pancetta is quite widely available from delicatessens or upmarket supermarkets but, if you have difficulty in tracking it down, use a smoked fatty streaky bacon, sliced wafer thin, instead. All you need to serve alongside is some French bread and a glass or two of crisp white wine.

baby monkfish tails in pancetta on ratatouille

Serves 4

4 baby or 2 large monkfish tails

100g cooking pancetta, sliced wafer thin

about 90ml olive oil

2 large red peppers, quartered

2 large yellow peppers, quartered

1 small red or white onion, thickly sliced

4–6 large garlic cloves, chopped

1 small aubergine, cut in 4 lengthways

1 large courgette, cut in 6 lengthways

leaves from 2 large sprigs fresh
  tarragon, chopped

6–8 large fresh basil leaves,
  roughly shredded

6 ripe plum tomatoes, skinned,
  de-seeded and roughly chopped

sea salt and freshly ground black pepper

Recommended wine: light Italian
  Barbera

1   Remove the grey membrane from the monkfish tails. If using large tails, fillet them and leave the 4 fillets separate. Fillet baby tails too, but put the pairs of fillets back together, running in opposite directions to each other. Season lightly and tightly wrap the pancetta around each of the baby monkfish tails or fillets. Set aside in the fridge to firm a little while you prepare the vegetables.

2   Preheat the oven to 200°C/400°F/Gas Mark 6. Heat a large flameproof baking pan on top of the stove until very hot. Add 1–2 tablespoons of the oil and heat. Add the monkfish tails and cook for 3–5 minutes until well browned on all sides. Transfer the monkfish tails to a plate.

3   Add the remaining oil to the pan and heat well. Sauté the peppers and onion over a medium heat for 3–5 minutes. Add the garlic, aubergine and courgette. Cook for a further 5 minutes until nicely coloured, then stir in the tarragon, basil, tomatoes and seasoning. Mix well, then place the monkfish tails on top.

4   Place the pan in the oven and cook for 8–10 minutes. Remove from the oven and stir the vegetables around the fish. Return to the oven if anything needs a little more cooking, but take care not to overcook the monkfish; it should feel firm but still a little springy when pressed. When cooked, allow to stand in a warm place for about 5 minutes before serving.

My fishcakes are made with a creamy potato purée and uncooked salmon so that the fish stays juicy, then coated with rich brioche crumbs: proof that the minimum of ingredients can produce the best results. If you can't get hold of brioche, then use dried breadcrumbs or even ground grissini. Watercress or spinach can be substituted for the sorrel, if necessary.

salmon fishcakes with sorrel sauce

1   Put the potatoes in a saucepan and just cover with lightly salted water. Boil for 12–15 minutes or until tender, then drain. Return to the pan and dry off over a gentle heat for a minute or so. Mash the flesh until smooth, preferably using a potato ricer. Beat in the butter, chervil, chives and seasoning. Set aside to cool and firm up.

2   Blend one-quarter of the salmon in a food processor until you have a smooth purée, scraping down the sides of the container once or twice. Chop the remaining fish into very fine dice. Mix the salmon purée into the cooled mashed potatoes. Mix in the egg yolk and then the diced fish. Lightly dust your hands with flour to prevent sticking, then shape the mixture into six round cakes.

3   Beat the whole egg in a shallow bowl. Tip the brioche crumbs into another shallow bowl. Dip all the fishcakes into the egg, coating well, then dip them into the crumbs, shaking off any excess. Put the fishcakes on a large plate and chill for at least 30 minutes to set the coating.

4   Meanwhile, prepare the sauce. Reheat the fish velouté to just below boiling. Remove from the heat and stir in the sorrel and lemon juice. Leave to infuse.

5   Heat the clarified butter or sunflower oil with the 2 tablespoons of oil in a shallow pan until hot, but not burning. Slide the fishcakes into the pan, one at a time, using a fish slice. Cook over a medium heat for about 5 minutes. Carefully turn and cook the other side for another 5 minutes until golden brown and crisp.

6   Drain on kitchen paper towels but do not cover or the fishcakes will become soggy. Reheat the sauce and serve with the fishcakes.

Makes 6

400g floury potatoes (Desirée or King
   Edward), peeled and diced
15g butter
1 tsp chopped fresh chervil
1 tsp chopped fresh chives
500g skinned salmon fillet
1 large egg + 1 yolk
100g dried brioche crumbs (page 218)
75g clarified butter (page 218)
   + 2 tbsp sunflower oil for frying (or
   use 150ml sunflower oil)
sea salt and freshly ground black pepper

For the sauce:

250ml Fish Velouté with Cream or
   without Cream (page 62)
40g fresh sorrel leaves, finely shredded
2 tsp fresh lemon juice

Alternative fish: cod, haddock, hoki,
   orange roughy
Recommended wine: white Rully

A mixture of fish makes for an interesting pie. I often use offcuts from other recipes, but you could also use a selection of perhaps three fish, ideally choosing those with a good range of different flavours and textures, such as firm monkfish, salmon and flaky cod. This recipe is enriched with mushrooms, shallots and velouté sauce, then topped with a deliciously buttery puff pastry.

a simple fish pie

Serves 4

2 tbsp olive oil

1 shallot, finely chopped

100g button mushrooms, quartered

250g homemade or good-quality
  ready-made puff pastry

600g skinned fish fillets (e.g. a mixture
  of salmon, cod and monkfish), cut
  into chunks

2 tbsp chopped fresh chervil

1 tbsp chopped fresh chives

250ml Fish Velouté with or without
  Cream (page 62), cooled

1 egg yolk beaten with 1 tsp water

sea salt and freshly ground black pepper

Alternative fish: red mullet, sea bass,
  sole, turbot

Recommended wine: an Austrian
  Sylvaner

1   Heat the oil in a small saucepan and gently sauté the shallot for 5 minutes, or until softened. Stir in the mushrooms and cook for another 5 minutes. Set aside to cool.

2   Roll out the pastry about 2cm larger all round than the top of a 1.5 litre pie dish with a lipped edge. Trim off a 1cm ring of pastry all round; you will need this later to line the rim of the dish. Set aside.

3   Place the fish chunks in the pie dish. Scatter over the chervil and chives and season with 1 teaspoon of salt and some pepper to taste. Spoon over the shallot and mushroom mix, then the fish velouté. Mix gently together.

4   Brush the rim of the pie dish with a little of the egg yolk glaze. Press the 1cm ring of pastry on to the edge and brush with a little more of the glaze. Using the rolling pin to help, lift the rolled-out pastry up and place over the filling. Press the edges well to seal, then trim off excess pastry with a sharp knife and pinch the edge to crimp. Brush with the egg glaze and cut a cross in the centre, then put the pie in the fridge to set for 30 minutes.

5   Preheat the oven to 200°C/400°F/Gas Mark 6. Remove the pie from the fridge and place on a baking sheet. Bake for 20–25 minutes, or until the pastry is golden brown and crisp, and the filling cooked through and bubbling. Allow the pie to stand for about 10 minutes before serving.

I enjoy making fish versions of popular classical dishes. This version of the traditional spicy sausage and goose dish from Toulouse can be made with any selection of firm-fleshed fish. The choice is entirely up to you. In fact, you can add or subtract whatever ingredients you like – that is the beauty of a cassoulet.

seafood cassoulet with haricot beans

Serves 4

300g skinned fish fillets (e.g. salmon, monkfish and sea bass)

1 small squid, prepared

about 6 tbsp olive oil

150g raw langoustines or tiger prawns, peeled

6 medium scallops, shelled and cleaned

50g smoked bacon, chopped

1 medium onion, chopped

2 tbsp chopped bulb fennel

3 tbsp dry white wine (optional)

⅙ Savoy cabbage, thickly shredded

4 ripe plum tomatoes, skinned, de-seeded and chopped

1 tsp tomato purée

150g cooked haricot beans (from 50g dried beans) or 420g can cannellini beans, rinsed and drained

300ml Fish Stock (pages 58–59)

100ml double cream

about 1 tsp chopped fresh parsley

sea salt and freshly ground black pepper

Recommended wine: a light red St Joseph Rhône valley

1   Remove any pin bones from the fish fillets, using tweezers if necessary. Cut the flesh into chunks. Slice the squid tubes into rings.

2   In a large shallow saucepan, heat half the oil. Sauté the fish, squid rings and tentacles, langoustines or tiger prawns and scallops for about 3 minutes. Cook in batches, gently stirring with a palette knife and taking care not to overcook. The squid will be cooked when it just turns white and the prawns just as they become pink. When cooked, transfer to a plate. Preheat the oven to 180°C/350°F/Gas Mark 4.

3   Add the remaining oil to the pan and sauté the bacon, onion and fennel for 3–5 minutes, until softened and nicely coloured. Pour in the wine, if using, and cook until it evaporates. Stir in the cabbage, chopped tomatoes and tomato purée. Cook for a further 5 minutes until the tomatoes start to soften. Stir in the haricot or cannellini beans, stock and seasoning. Bring to the boil, then remove from the heat and stir in the cream. Pour into a shallow casserole.

4   Place the cooked seafood on top. Stir gently into the bean mixture without immersing it completely. Cover lightly with foil and cook in the oven for 10–15 minutes. Sprinkle lightly with a little chopped parsley and serve.

Fish and cabbage make fine plate fellows, and pink salmon served on pale green cabbage speckled with fresh herbs is especially delicious. Buy salmon fillets cut from the thick part of the fish so that you have good chunky 'steaks' to work with. Choose a pale green spring or pointed variety of cabbage for this dish. Serve with a salad of baby spinach leaves and perhaps some new potatoes.

pan-roasted salmon on creamy cabbage

1   Check the salmon fillets for any pin bones and trim to neaten, if necessary.

2   Bring a large pan of water to the boil and blanch the cabbage for just 30 seconds. Drain and refresh under cold running water. Drain well again and set aside.

3   Heat the butter or oil in the same pan and gently sauté the shallot for 3 minutes. Add the blanched cabbage and cook for another 3 minutes, stirring occasionally.

4   Add the vinegar and cook, stirring, until evaporated, then pour in the wine and cook until reduced by half. Stir in the cream and bring to the boil, then season to taste. Remove from the heat, cover and keep warm while you cook the fish.

5   Heat a large non-stick frying pan. When really hot, add the 1 teaspoon of oil and swirl it around. Reduce the heat to medium, then cook the salmon fillets for about 3 minutes on each side, or until they still feel lightly springy. Take care not to overcook. Season to taste with salt and pepper.

6   Stir the chopped chives, parsley and chervil into the creamed cabbage mixture. Divide the cabbage among four warmed dinner plates and sit the salmon fillets on top. Garnish with sprigs of chervil and serve.

Serves 4

4 x 200g salmon fillets, skinned

½ large pale green cabbage,
   finely shredded

40g butter or 2 tbsp olive oil
   + 1 tsp olive oil for the fish

1 shallot, finely chopped

2 tsp sherry vinegar

75ml Chardonnay or other
   dry white wine

90ml double cream

1 tbsp chopped fresh chives

1 tbsp chopped fresh flat-leaf parsley

1 tbsp chopped fresh chervil + sprigs
   to garnish

sea salt and freshly ground black pepper

Alternative fish: cod, grouper, haddock,
   hoki, orange roughy

Recommended wine: white Vouvray

You can turn a meaty fillet of cod into something even better by adding a mildly spicy mushroom topping and a herb crust. The method used here for putting the crust on each fillet is quite ingenious. The cod is delicious served on top of some wilted spinach, with Spiced Rice Pilaff (page 198) and a velouté sauce.

cod with a butter herb crust

1   Heat the oil in a saucepan and add the mushrooms. Cook until sizzling, then reduce the heat and gently sauté for about 10 minutes, until they soften into a chunky purée. If the mushrooms produce a lot of liquid as they cook, raise the heat to evaporate it. Season and set aside.

2   Meanwhile, purée the tomatoes in a food processor. Remove and set aside.

3   For the herb crust, finely chop the herbs in the food processor, then add the butter and blend again. Tip in the breadcrumbs and blend to a paste. Scrape out on to a sheet of cling film or foil. Using a palette knife, spread the paste into a rectangular shape large enough to cover the four fillets. Cover with another layer of cling film or foil. Roll lightly with a rolling pin to smooth the top. Chill for about 2 hours until firm.

4   Preheat the oven to 200°C/400°F/Gas Mark 6. Remove the herb crust from the fridge and pull off the top layer of cling film or foil. Cut into four rectangles to fit the fillets. Spread the top of each fillet with mustard. Spoon over the tomato purée and cover with the mushrooms. Place a rectangle of herb crust on top of each fillet, then place on a baking tray.

5   Bake the fish for about 15 minutes, or until the flesh just starts to flake. While the fish is cooking, preheat the grill to hot. Remove the fish from the oven and place under the grill to crisp up the herb crust. Serve straight away.

Serves 4

1 tbsp olive oil

100g button mushrooms, very
    finely chopped

2 ripe plum tomatoes, skinned and
    de-seeded

4 x 150g chunky cod fillets, skinned

1 tbsp whole-grained mustard

sea salt and freshly ground black pepper

For the herb crust:

40g fresh curly-leaf parsley,
    stalks discarded

1 tsp fresh thyme tips

50g butter, softened

150g fresh breadcrumbs

Alternative fish: thick-cut haddock fillets

Recommended wine: Aligoté

This recipe has all the hallmarks of a sunny Mediterranean dish – plump, firm fish and fresh, lemon-scented vegetables. All the ingredients are cooked together in a large cast-iron casserole to draw out their flavours and enhance their colours. This is wonderful served with baby new potatoes and a peppery rocket salad topped with shavings of Parmesan cheese.

summer braised swordfish

Serves 4

3 tbsp olive oil

2 medium onions, sliced in rings

12 small shallots, halved

8 plum tomatoes, skinned, de-seeded and quartered

3–4 courgettes, thinly sliced

2 bay leaves

large sprig fresh thyme

2 stalks lemon grass, each cut in 3

400ml Chardonnay or other dry white wine

4 x 150g swordfish steaks

sea salt and freshly ground black pepper

Alternative fish: chunky cod fillets

Recommended wine: a light Merlot

1   Preheat the oven to 200°C/400°F/Gas Mark 6. Place an empty cast-iron casserole in the oven until hot, then add the olive oil and move to the top of the cooker. Add the onions, shallots, tomatoes, courgettes, bay leaves, thyme and lemon grass, and season. Cook, uncovered, stirring occasionally, for about 15 minutes, or until the vegetables start to caramelize.

2   Pour in the wine, then return to the oven and cook for about 10 minutes or until the liquid has reduced by half.

3   Place the swordfish steaks on top of the vegetables. Spoon over the sauce to coat the fish, and lightly season. Return to the oven and cook for 10–12 minutes until the fish feels just firm when pressed gently.

4   Remove the fish from the casserole. Spoon the vegetables on to four warmed dinner plates. Set the swordfish carefully on top of the vegetables. Trickle over the pan juices and serve.

This simple and unusual recipe is ideal for cooking in the autumn, when fresh figs appear in the shops and lemon sole are plump. The confit can be made in advance, then added just before cooking the fish. Delicious with Spiced Rice Pilaff (page 198), or with couscous and Fresh Harissa (page 70).

sole with fig and lemon confit

1   Preheat the oven to 190°C/375°F/Gas Mark 5. Halve the figs lengthways and arrange in a shallow baking dish. Top with the lemon slices and drizzle over 2 tablespoons of the olive oil.

2   Cover the dish with foil and bake for about 30 minutes, until the figs reduce down and are soft and juicy. Remove from the oven and set the dish to one side until you are ready to cook the fish.

3   Brush another shallow baking or roasting dish with the remaining oil. Place the sole fillets in the dish in a single layer. Season well. Spoon over the lemony figs with their juices and, maybe, an extra trickle of olive oil.

4   Bake, uncovered, for about 15 minutes or until the flesh of the lemon sole feels just firm when pressed with a fork. Serve straight away.

Serves 4

8 firm fresh figs
1 lemon, thinly sliced
3 tbsp olive oil
4 x 300–400g lemon sole,
   filleted and skinned
sea salt and coarsely ground
   black pepper

Alternative fish: plaice, whiting
Recommended wine: South African
   Gewürztraminer

A paella is a wonderful celebration of seafood, chicken, vegetables and rice all cooked together with paprika, garlic and, of course, saffron. It's important to have a good mix of seafood, although anything you can't find can be replaced with something similar, or left out altogether.

seafood paella

Serves 6–8

1.5 litres Chicken Stock (page 61)

1 small to medium chicken, cooked

2 x 200g lobster tails, cooked

200g small squid, prepared

500g fresh mussels, de-bearded

1 x 200g monkfish tail, filleted

5 tbsp olive oil

1 medium onion, finely chopped

1 medium leek, thinly sliced

½ small red pepper, chopped

½ small green pepper, chopped

6 ripe plum tomatoes, skinned,
   de-seeded and chopped

2 large cloves garlic, crushed

½ tsp saffron strands

1 bay leaf

500g paella or Arborio rice

150ml dry white wine

200g raw langoustines or tiger prawns,
   peeled but last tail section left on

1 tsp paprika

chopped fresh parsley to garnish

sea salt and freshly ground black pepper

Recommended wine: Spanish white
   Grenache

1   Prepare all the ingredients before you start cooking. Heat the chicken stock in a pan. Cut the cooked chicken into 8 joints using poultry shears or a heavy sharp knife. Discard the wing and leg tips and the back. Shell the lobster tails and cut the meat into chunks. Cut the squid tubes into rings, reserving the tentacles. Pick over the mussels and discard any that are open. Cut the monkfish fillets into chunks.

2   Heat half the oil in a paella pan or a large, shallow pan of 5 litre capacity. Sauté the onion, leek, peppers, tomatoes and garlic with the saffron and bay leaf for 5–10 minutes, or until the vegetables are softened. Stir in the rice and cook for 3–5 minutes, stirring, until it turns opaque. Stir in the wine to de-glaze and cook until evaporated.

3   Ladle in the hot stock, allowing each amount to be absorbed before adding the next, and stirring very occasionally. Cooking should take about 15 minutes. When the rice has been cooking for about 10 minutes, add the mussels.

4   In the meantime, heat the remaining oil in a frying pan and sauté the monkfish chunks for about 3 minutes, stirring; remove. Add the squid rings and tentacles, the lobster pieces and langoustines or prawns. Stir until the langoustines or prawns just turn pink and feel firm. Take care not to overcook the seafood.

5   Stir all the cooked seafood and chicken pieces into the rice. Season with salt and pepper, then sprinkle over the paprika and mix in gently along with any remaining stock. (If the rice still seems a little chalky and undercooked, you can add some boiling water and cook for a further 6–8 minutes, or until everything is ready and the rice is plump.) Scatter over the parsley and serve accompanied by salad and crusty bread.

A rather luxurious variation on the classic moules marinières, this is the perfect dish for a supper with style. Prepare all the vegetables and other ingredients before you tackle the mussels so that they are cooked from as fresh a state as possible. I recommend scrubbing and then de-bearding them just before cooking so they don't open until they hit the pot.

mussels with creamy winter vegetables

1   Scrub the mussels, discarding any that are open. Just before cooking, pull off the wispy beards from those tightly closed. As soon as you finish de-bearding, heat a large, heavy-based saucepan until very hot. Add the mussels, thyme, bay leaf and one-third of the wine. Cover and heat for a minute or two, then shake the pan well.

2   Place back on the heat and remove the lid. Stir the mussels almost continuously for 3–4 minutes. When they have all opened, drain in a colander set over a bowl to save the cooking liquid. Discard any closed mussels and the bay leaf. Remove the mussels from their shells and discard the shells. Keep the mussels warm.

3   In the same saucepan, melt the butter and add the leek, fennel, mushrooms, shallots, curry powder and star anise. Cover the pan and gently sweat the vegetables for about 7 minutes, or until softened but not coloured. Add the remaining wine and bring to the boil. Cook, uncovered, until the cooking liquid has almost completely evaporated. Remove the star anise.

4   Add the mussel liquor. Cook, uncovered, for 5 minutes to reduce again. Add the cream and parsley and bring back to the boil. Sprinkle in the saffron, heat for 1–2 minutes and season to taste. Mix the mussels with the vegetable mixture and divide among four warmed soup bowls.

Serves 2

1.5kg fresh mussels

2 tsp fresh thyme tips

1 bay leaf

300ml dry white wine

50g unsalted butter

1 small leek, finely sliced

½ bulb fennel, sliced into julienne

200g brown chestnut mushrooms or
    Champignons de Paris, finely sliced

4 shallots, finely chopped

pinch curry powder

2 star anise

100ml double cream

4 sprigs fresh flat-leaf parsley,
    finely chopped

pinch saffron strands

sea salt and freshly ground black pepper

Recommended wine: Muscadet

dinner party fish

This recipe uses a simple technique to turn fillets of halibut into a special dish – strips of smoked salmon are threaded through the fillets, using a larding needle (you can buy one from most kitchen equipment stores). The strips are best cut from a chunk of partially frozen, unsliced salmon so they are easier to thread. The simple and delicious sauce is a favourite of one of my mentors, Albert Roux, who taught me so much.

halibut larded with smoked salmon and sauce albert

Serves 4

200g smoked salmon, in one piece

4 x 150g halibut fillets, skinned

good knob of butter

100g baby onions, peeled and left whole

1 Cos lettuce, shredded

250g shelled peas, fresh or frozen

1 tbsp olive oil

For the sauce:

1 tbsp olive oil

2 shallots, finely chopped

25g fresh horseradish, peeled and
  grated, or 2 tbsp horseradish relish

2 tbsp dry white wine

150ml double cream

2 tsp fresh lemon juice

sea salt and freshly ground black pepper

Alternative fish: thick fillets of turbot

Recommended wine: Meursault

1   Partially freeze the salmon, then cut into 16 long, thin strips, each about 5mm x 10cm. Trim each halibut fillet into a neat rectangle. Grip a strip of salmon in a larding needle and pull the strip through a halibut fillet lengthways. Repeat three times. Pull four strips of salmon through each of the remaining fillets in the same way. Trim the edges, then set aside in the fridge.

2   Make the sauce: in a saucepan, heat the oil and gently sauté the shallots with the fresh horseradish, if using, for about 5 minutes, or until softened but not coloured. Add the wine and cook for a minute or two until almost evaporated. Pour in the cream, adding the horseradish relish, if using, and season. Bring to the boil, then simmer for 2 minutes. Strain through a sieve. Check the seasoning and add the lemon juice. Strain into a small saucepan and set aside to reheat later.

3   Heat the butter with about 3 tablespoons of water in a saucepan. Add the baby onions and cook for about 5 minutes until softened. Add the shredded lettuce, and stir. Cover and cook for about 3 minutes until wilted. Add the peas and cook for another 3 minutes, then season to taste. Drain and set aside.

4   Now, cook the fish. In a large non-stick frying pan, heat the oil and pan-fry the fillets for about 3 minutes on each side until just cooked. Season lightly on each side. Reheat the sauce and the vegetables to serve with the fish.

The concept for this dish is both simple and extraordinary: neat pieces of a variety of contrasting fish served on a red wine sauce flavoured with five-spice powder. It is a dish that breaks with convention, and its impact is not just in the contrast of colours, but also in the different shapes of the fish pieces.

navarin of fish with five-spice sauce

Serves 4

600g selection of fish fillets (e.g. red
   mullet, salmon, sea bass, turbot,
   monkfish and scallops)

200g fresh linguine or tagliatelle

150g baby spinach leaves

30g butter

1 tbsp olive oil

250ml Fish Velouté with Cream
   (page 62) to serve (optional)

2 tsp chopped fresh chives

sea salt and freshly ground black pepper

For the red wine sauce:

1 bottle red wine

2 tbsp olive oil

6 large shallots, finely chopped

1 tsp five-spice powder

½ tsp black peppercorns or Sichuan
   red peppercorns

1 sprig fresh thyme

1 small bay leaf

1 tbsp sherry vinegar

800ml Chicken Stock (page 61)

Recommended wine: Tasmanian
   Pinot Noir

1   To make the sauce, boil the red wine down to about 150ml and set aside. Meanwhile, in another saucepan, heat the oil and gently sauté the shallots with the five-spice powder, peppercorns, thyme and bay leaf for about 10 minutes. Pour in the sherry vinegar and cook until almost evaporated. Stir in the reduced red wine and the stock. Boil again for about 20 minutes, or until reduced by half. Strain twice through a sieve lined with muslin, to produce a smooth, rich sauce. Set aside.

2   Skin turbot and monkfish, but leave the skin on mullet, salmon and sea bass. Trim all the fish to neat, bite-sized shapes such as diamonds, squares or ovals. Make a good mixture without too much waste.

3   Cook the linguine or tagliatelle in plenty of salted boiling water for a minute or two until just al dente. Drain. In another pan, cook the spinach in a tiny amount of boiling water for a minute until just wilted. Put both the pasta and the spinach in a sieve and refresh under cold running water. Drain well and set aside. Prepare two saucepans, each containing half the butter plus a few tablespoons of seasoned water.

4   In a large non-stick frying pan, heat the oil and cook the pieces of fish, turning once, for no longer than 5 minutes or until lightly firm. Season in the pan and keep warm. Using the two pans of buttery water, reheat the pasta in one and the spinach in the other for 1– 2 minutes, then drain well. Reheat the red wine sauce and cream velouté if using.

5   Spoon a small mound of spinach into the centre of four warmed dinner plates. Toss the pasta with the chopped chives. Using a large serving fork, wind one-quarter of the pasta around the prongs, then slip off on to each spinach mound. Spoon the red wine sauce around the pasta and place the fish on the sauce. Trickle over some of the cream velouté, if using. Serve as soon as possible.

Silvery sea bass is one of my favourite fish and, now that it is farmed, it is becoming easier to find. If by any chance you come across small bass of one-portion size, then make up four individual servings and grill or barbecue the fish for 7–10 minutes on each side.

roasted sea bass with fennel and ginger

1   If possible, leave the head on the fish as it helps to hold the stuffing in place and the finished dish will look more attractive. Check to be sure that the blood line inside the body cavity has been washed out.

2   Heat the oil in a saucepan and lightly sauté the shallot, fennel and ginger for about 7 minutes until softened. Pour in the wine and cook until completely evaporated. Season, then remove from the heat to cool.

3   Preheat the oven to 190°C/375°F/Gas Mark 5. Spoon the filling into the bass, pressing it down and shaping the fish around it. Using a sharp knife, lightly score the skin two or three times on each side. Place the fish in a shallow ovenproof dish, brush the skin with a little oil and season.

4   Roast the fish for 20–25 minutes, or until it feels just firm when pressed at the thickest part; check by opening a little slit along the backbone and pressing the flesh. During cooking, brush with a little more oil to keep moist. Towards the end of cooking, drizzle over the lemon juice.

5   Remove from the oven and allow to stand for 5 minutes. Then, using a sharp, thin-bladed knife, cut along one side of the backbone and work your way down along the rib cage until you have one long fillet. Repeat on the other side. Cut the fillets in two. Spoon the filling on to four warmed plates and rest the fish, skin side up, on top. Trickle any pan juices over the fish. Garnish with the reserved fennel fronds and serve.

Serves 4

1 whole sea bass, about 1kg, gutted
    and trimmed
2 tbsp olive oil + a little extra for brushing
1 shallot, finely chopped
1 medium bulb fennel, finely chopped
    + fronds to garnish
1 tbsp finely chopped fresh ginger
150ml dry white wine
juice ½ small lemon
sea salt and freshly ground black pepper

Alternative fish: brill or cod
Recommended wine: an Alsace Tokay

Although a member of the bream family, the dorade royale (gilt-head bream) looks more like a snapper. It makes excellent eating, especially when cooked in the Mediterranean style – grilled, then served on a bed of spiced couscous with apples and sultanas. The scales of this fish can be rather sharp, so ask your fishmonger to remove them for you.

dorade royale with spicy couscous

1   Soak the sultanas in warm water for 10 minutes to plump, then drain and pat dry. In a bowl, pour 200ml boiling water over the couscous. Mix in the rock salt and 2 teaspoons of the olive oil. Leave to soak for 1 hour, stirring occasionally to break up any lumps, until the grains are separate and fluffy.

2   Mix the sultanas, chilli spice mix, apple and chopped coriander into the couscous and season. Just before you are ready to cook the fish, either steam the couscous for 8–10 minutes, stirring once or twice with a fork, or cover and reheat in a microwave oven on full power for 4 minutes, stirring once. Keep the couscous warm while you cook the fish.

3   Preheat the grill until very hot. Check the fish fillets for any pin bones and remove with tweezers. Score the skin side of each fillet two or three times. Rub with a little oil, then press two candied lemon slices on the skin of each fillet. Sprinkle over the rosemary and season. Grill, skin side up, for about 5 minutes until crispy. There is no need to turn the fish. Keep warm.

4   Mix the lemon zest and juice into the vinaigrette. Divide the couscous between two plates. Drizzle with the remaining oil.

5   Lightly season the fish, then place a fillet over each couscous mound. Drizzle over the vinaigrette and garnish with the thyme or coriander sprigs, either deep-fried or fresh, and serve straight away.

Serves 2

1 tbsp sultanas

100g couscous

½ tsp crushed rock salt

3 tbsp olive oil

1 tsp Chilli Spice Mix (page 74)

½ Granny Smith apple, peeled and chopped

2 tsp chopped fresh coriander

1 dorade royale, about 650g, scaled and filleted in two

4 Candied Lemon slices (page 216)

1 tsp chopped fresh rosemary

½ tsp grated lemon zest

2 tsp fresh lemon juice

2 tbsp Classic Vinaigrette (page 76)

deep-fried or fresh sprigs thyme or coriander to garnish

sea salt and freshly ground black pepper

Alternative fish: red mullet, salmon

Recommended wines: South Australian Chardonnay, white Châteauneuf-du-Pape or a Provençal white wine, e.g. Bandol

Red wine suits the robust flavour of turbot, and poaching fillets of turbot in reduced red wine gives them a deep burgundy skin which makes a stunning contrast in colour with their creamy white flesh. The red wine poaching liquid can be reused for other poaching. You can serve the turbot, coated in its sauce, with some lightly cooked asparagus spears or baby leeks, or with spinach dressed with a little butter.

turbot in red wine with civet sauce

Serves 4

1 litre red wine

1 tbsp olive oil

2 shallots, finely chopped

100ml Fish Stock (pages 58–59)

400ml Claret Sauce (page 63)

500g potatoes, peeled and diced

good knob of butter

2–3 tbsp hot milk

4 x 200g turbot fillets, skinned and
   neatly trimmed

sea salt and freshly ground black pepper

Alternative fish: cod, haddock, halibut,
   grouper

Recommended wine: a red Burgundy
   Pinot Noir, e.g. Monthélie

1   Boil the red wine until reduced by half.

2   Heat the oil in a saucepan and gently cook the shallots for about 10 minutes until softened. Pour in about 4 tablespoons of the reduced red wine. Cook until reduced further, to a syrupy glaze. Add the stock and cook for about 10 minutes, or until reduced by half. Pour in the claret sauce and bring to the boil. Cook uncovered for 20 minutes. Strain through a fine sieve into a clean pan and keep warm.

3   While the sauce is simmering, in another saucepan boil the potatoes until tender. Drain and return to the hot empty pan, then cook for a minute or two to dry off. Mash until smooth and creamy, using a potato ricer if you have one. Add the butter and hot milk, and beat into a creamy purée that holds its shape. Season well and keep warm.

4   In a large heavy-based saucepan, bring the remaining reduced red wine to the boil and season lightly. Add the turbot fillets. Return to a gentle boil, then reduce the heat to a very gentle simmer. Cook for about 10 minutes, or until the flesh feels just firm when pressed. Remove with a fish slice and season lightly once more.

5   Spoon the potato purée on to four warmed dinner plates. (For a smart presentation, you can shape it into smooth rounds using a large plain cutter.) Place the turbot fillets on top, coat with the warm civet sauce and serve.

I have something of a soft spot for John Dory, with their distinctive St Peter's thumbprint and their individual charm. They are a cross between a flat fish and a round fish, and delicious in flavour, but they do need to be filleted with care. Bear in mind that you will lose a lot in the filleting as the head is so large. If you doubt your knife skills, then ask the fishmonger to carry out this task. To serve, I suggest a creamy Fish Velouté (page 62) flavoured with some shredded fresh tarragon, or Sauce Maltaise (page 66).

john dory with caramelized chicory

1   Check the fillets for any pin bones and trim the edges. Set aside in the fridge.

2   Fill a pan with water and add the lemon juice, 1 tablespoon of the sugar and ½ teaspoon of salt. Bring to the boil, then add the chicory and simmer for about 8 minutes. Drain well and leave until cool enough to handle, then gently squeeze the heads to remove any excess water. Sprinkle with the remaining sugar and season to taste. Leave for 10 minutes.

3   Heat the butter in a shallow, medium-sized pan. When the butter is hot but not burning, add the chicory heads and cook for 3–4 minutes until light brown and caramelized on all sides.

4   Tip in a little of the nage, stock or water. Shake the pan until the liquid is blended with the pan juices. Cook over a medium heat until the liquid evaporates, then drizzle in a little more. Continue like this until all the liquid has been added and the chicory heads are softened. They should appear glossy and golden brown. Keep warm.

5   In a large frying pan, heat the oil and fry the fish fillets for about 2 minutes on each side. Season to taste and serve with the chicory heads.

Serves 4

4 John Dory, about 400g each, filleted and skinned

1 tbsp fresh lemon juice

3 tbsp caster sugar

4 large heads chicory, cored and trimmed

25g butter

150ml Vegetable Nage (page 61), Fish Stock (pages 58–59) or water

1 tbsp olive oil

sea salt and freshly ground black pepper

Alternative fish: large red mullet
Recommended wine: a dry Alsace Muscat

Long, thin slices of potato are wrapped around fillets of brill and cooked to an appetizing crispiness in this impressive dinner party dish. It does take a little time to put together, but certain parts of the recipe can be done in advance. If you have the time and feel like pushing the boat out, you can also make up some Claret Sauce (page 63) to drizzle around the fish parcels.

brill wrapped in crispy potatoes with a fondue of leeks

Serves 6

4 x 150g brill fillets, skinned

2–3 large waxy potatoes, ideally long and evenly shaped, peeled

150g clarified butter (page 218)

1–2 tbsp olive oil

2 large leeks, very finely chopped

about ½ tsp curry powder

4 tbsp dry white wine

200ml single cream

sea salt and freshly ground black pepper

Alternative fish: halibut, salmon, thick sole fillets

Recommended wine: Australian Sémillon

1   Check the brill fillets for any pin bones, and remove with tweezers. Trim the fillets to even-sized tranches (page 31). Lightly season and set aside.

2   Using a swivel vegetable peeler, or mandolin, cut long shavings of potato. The slices should be even and thin enough to fold without snapping, but not so thin that they become translucent.

3   Heat half the clarified butter with half the oil in a frying pan until hot but not smoking. Blanch the potato strips in the fat, a few at a time, for about 2 minutes until just softened but not coloured. (You may need to replace the butter and oil occasionally if it starts to burn.) As the potato strips are cooked, keep them warm so that they do not harden.

4   Wrap each brill fillet in potato strips, overlapping each strip by half, to make four neatly wrapped parcels. (You may need to use 2 potato strips per row, depending on the thickness of the fish.) Place in the fridge to chill and set for 1 hour. Remove and brush lightly with a little more clarified butter, then return to the fridge.

5   Heat about 2 tablespoons of clarified butter in a saucepan and gently cook the chopped leeks for 5–7 minutes until softened. Just before they are done, add the curry powder and stir well. Stir in the wine and cook for 2 minutes. Season and pour in the cream. Simmer for a further 5 minutes to reduce. Keep warm.

6   Heat a large non-stick frying pan. When hot, add the fish parcels to the dry pan. Cook for about 3 minutes on each side until brown and crisp. Drain on kitchen paper towels. Spoon small mounds of the leek fondue on to serving plates and place the fish parcels on top. Serve immediately.

This is a light dish, ideal for autumn with its mellow flavours and rich golden colours. Fillets of red mullet are poached in a light vegetable nage and the liquid used for a juniper sauce. Choucroute (or sauerkraut), which can be bought in cans or jars, has an assertive flavour so you don't need very much. Alternatively, you may prefer to use finely shredded and blanched green cabbage.

red mullet with choucroute and juniper berry sauce

Serves 4

4 x 400g red mullet, filleted and skin on

1 carrot, sliced into julienne

4 tbsp choucroute or sauerkraut

30g butter

500ml Vegetable Nage (page 61)

12 juniper berries, lightly crushed

3 tbsp double cream

fresh parsley or chervil sprigs to garnish

sea salt and freshly ground black pepper

Alternative fish: mackerel, skate wings

Recommended wine: white Graves

1   Check the fish fillets for pin bones and remove with tweezers. Trim the edges of the fillets neatly. (You can cut the fillets into diamond shapes, for an impressive presentation, but this is not necessary.)

2   In a saucepan, bring a little salted water to the boil and blanch the carrot julienne for 2 minutes. Drain and return to the pan. Add the choucroute, half the butter and a tablespoon or two of water. Set aside ready for reheating.

3   Pour the nage into a wide, shallow pan. Add the crushed juniper berries, bring to the boil and simmer for a minute or two. Slide in the mullet fillets and poach for about 5 minutes until just firm.

4   Remove the fillets with a fish slice and keep warm. Bring the nage back to the boil and cook until reduced by half. Strain through a fine sieve, then return to the pan.

5   While the nage is reducing, reheat the carrot and choucroute mixture until just boiling. Remove from the heat and keep warm.

6   Whisk the remaining butter and the cream into the reduced nage. Spoon the carrot and choucroute mixture into the middle of four warmed large bowls. Arrange two mullet fillets each on top. Spoon the sauce over the fish. Garnish with parsley or chervil sprigs and serve straight away.

The French Basque pipérade of sweet peppers, onions and tomatoes is normally cooked with eggs, like a scrambled omelette. This version uses fresh tuna steaks instead of eggs and a fresh herb sauce vierge, turning it into a main course. The vegetables and sauce are best served warm, slightly hotter than room temperature, so that the flavours are at their liveliest. The tuna steaks and Swiss chard can be served hot. If Swiss chard is not available, you can use full-grown spinach instead.

tuna pipérade with swiss chard

1   In a saucepan, heat 2 tablespoons of the oil and sauté the shallots for about 5 minutes until softened but not coloured. Add the peppers and cook for a further 3 minutes. Stir in the tomato concassé and season, then remove from the heat. Leave to cool until warm, then mix in the basil and set aside.

2   Lightly peel any tough parts from the chard stalks, then cut into 4cm wide slices. Roughly chop the chard leaves. Cook the stalks in lightly salted boiling water for 2 minutes. Add the leaves and return to the boil, then drain. Toss with the butter. Season and keep warm while you cook the fish.

3   Lightly season the tuna steaks. Heat a large non-stick frying pan and, when smoking hot, add the remaining oil. When the oil is hot, slip in the tuna steaks and pan-fry for 3 minutes or until nicely browned. Carefully turn over. Cook the other side for 2–3 minutes, until the steaks are just tender but still a little springy to the touch.

4   Place the buttery chard in the centre of four plates. Top each with a tuna steak and spoon the pipérade on top. Drizzle the sauce vierge around, garnish with a little chopped parsley and serve.

Serves 4

3 tbsp olive oil

2 shallots, finely chopped

1 red pepper, finely diced

1 yellow pepper, finely diced

2 plum tomatoes, concassé (page 218)

6 large leaves fresh basil, shredded

200g Swiss chard

good knob of butter

4 x 150g tuna steaks, preferably
   yellow fin

150ml Sauce Vierge (page 69)

1 tbsp chopped fresh parsley

sea salt and freshly ground black pepper

Recommended wine: a dry white
   wine from South-west France,
   e.g. Pacherenc du Vic-Bilh

A simple pan-fried fillet of fish is best set off with a clear-tasting sauce. In this case, bream is highlighted with a light fruit sauce spiked with shreds of citrus peel and basil. Make sure you cook the fish skin side down first so that the lucent pink skin is caramelized and shown to its best advantage. You can serve this dish with some lightly cooked green vegetables, such as mangetouts or sugar-snap peas.

pan-fried bream with a citrus and basil sauce

1   Check the fish for pin bones and remove any you find with tweezers. Neatly trim the edges of the fillets and set aside.

2   Using a canelle knife, take the zest from the orange, lemon, lime and grapefruit in fine strips. If you don't have a canelle knife, peel the zest thinly with a swivel vegetable peeler and cut in long, thin strips. Blanch the zest in a little boiling water for 2 minutes. Drain and refresh under cold running water, then pat dry. Set aside.

3   Cut all the peel and pith from the orange, lemon, lime and grapefruit. Using a small, sharp knife, cut segments from one half of each fruit, cutting the segments out from between the membranes. Hold the fruits over a bowl to catch the juices. Squeeze the juice from the remaining fruit halves and add to the bowl.

4   Pour the nage into a saucepan. Bring to the boil and continue boiling until reduced by half. Mix in the fruit segments and juices. Cook gently until the segments start to dissolve, lightly whisking for about 5 minutes. Season and set aside.

5   In a large non-stick frying pan, heat the oil and cook the fish, skin side down, for about 2 minutes, or until the skin is nicely caramelized. Carefully turn the fillets over and cook the other side for about 2 minutes, until the fish feels just firm. Season, then remove and keep warm.

6   Stir the blanched citrus zest into the sauce. Reheat for a minute or two, then whisk in the butter. Mix in the chervil and basil shreds. Divide the fillets among four plates and trickle over the sauce. Serve immediately.

Serves 4

4 x 400g bream, filleted and skin on

1 tbsp olive oil

sea salt and freshly ground black pepper

For the sauce:

1 large orange

1 lemon

1 lime

1 pink grapefruit

300ml Vegetable Nage (page 61)

small knob of butter

1 tbsp chopped fresh chervil

6 leaves fresh basil, cut in thin shreds

Alternative fish: red mullet

Recommended wine: Anjou Blanc

barbecues and casual occasions

These make a tasty starter for a party. The scallops can be cooked over the lingering embers of a barbecue, but avoid too fierce a heat as the bacon will toughen and the costly scallops burn. If you prefer not to prepare the scallops yourself, ask the fishmonger to do it for you and to supply you with just the chunky nuggets of meat. You will need 12 wooden satay sticks for this – soak them in cold water for a good half hour before cooking so they won't char too much.

scallops in smoky bacon jackets with rocket and parmesan salad

Serves 6

12 large scallops, shelled, trimmed
    and cleaned
12 rashers unsmoked back bacon,
    de-rinded
50g piece fresh Parmesan cheese
1–2 tbsp olive oil
about 250g rocket leaves
sea salt and freshly ground black pepper

For the dressing:

1 tsp English mustard powder
2 tbsp white wine vinegar
100ml single cream
good pinch caster sugar
2 tbsp chopped fresh chives

Alternative fish: cubes of monkfish
Recommended wine: Sicilian
    Chardonnay

1   Wrap each scallop in a rasher of bacon around the width, like a collar. (You may need to trim the streaky end a little for an even coat.) Skewer two wrapped scallops on to a pair of satay sticks (two parallel sticks are easier than single sticks to turn during cooking). Repeat with the rest of the wrapped scallops and doubled sticks.

2   Using a swivel vegetable peeler, cut shavings from half the Parmesan cheese and set aside. Finely grate the remainder. Make the dressing by whisking the mustard with the vinegar until smooth, then gradually whisk in the cream and grated Parmesan. Mix in the sugar and chives. Thin down a little with cold water to a light coating consistency.

3   Preheat the grill, or make your charcoal fire and let it burn down so it is not too hot. Brush the scallops all over with the oil. Season lightly. Grill or barbecue for 2 minutes on one side. Turn over and cook the other side for 1–2 minutes, or until lightly brown and just firm when pressed. Set aside while you make the salad.

4   Toss the rocket in the dressing and divide among six plates. Remove the sticks from the scallops. Place two scallops on each of the plates and scatter the Parmesan shavings on top. Serve immediately.

Thai cooking often calls for the most unlikely sounding combinations of pungent flavours, but the results are always spectacular. This Thai-inspired recipe is ideal for relaxed summer parties. Although the prawns need to be marinated in advance, they only take minutes to cook, and skewering them on wooden satay sticks before cooking makes them easier to turn. When you prepare the lemon grass for the dressing, be sure to peel off any dry-looking outer leaves before chopping.

barbecued tiger prawns with marinated tomatoes and thai-dressed salad

1   Peel and de-vein the tiger prawns, leaving the last tail section on.

2   Mix 150ml of the olive oil with the coriander seeds and curry powder, and stir in the prawns. Set aside to marinate in the fridge for at least 2 hours. If using wooden satay sticks, soak them in cold water for half an hour to prevent charring.

3   Cut the tomatoes in half and arrange in a heatproof dish, cut side up. Sprinkle with salt and brush with the remaining olive oil and the balsamic vinegar. Set aside until you are ready to cook.

4   Shake together all the ingredients for the dressing in a screw-top jar and chill for at least 2 hours. Put the salad leaves in a bowl and chill.

5   When ready to cook, thread the prawns on to the skewers. Make the fire in the barbecue, allowing enough time for the flames to die down to glowing embers before cooking. Alternatively, preheat the grill. Cook the tomatoes, cut side up, for about 3–5 minutes, or until soft and slightly charred. Barbecue or grill the prawns for about 3–4 minutes, until they turn bright pink all over, basting occasionally with the leftover marinade to keep them moist.

6   Shake up the dressing and toss with the salad leaves. Arrange on a large platter, place the tomatoes and prawns on the leaves, and serve.

Serves 6

24–30 raw tiger prawns

200ml olive oil

1 tbsp coriander seeds, lightly crushed

1 tsp mild curry powder

6 plum tomatoes

2 tbsp balsamic vinegar

about 300g mixed salad leaves

sea salt

For the dressing:

1 stalk fresh lemon grass, finely chopped

1 tbsp chopped fresh coriander

2 tbsp Thai fish sauce (nam pla)

1 tbsp light soy sauce

150ml sunflower oil

4 tbsp white wine vinegar or rice
  wine vinegar

Alternative fish: scallops or cubes
  of monkfish

Recommended wine: a dry Alsace
  Muscat

A darne is a cutlet of salmon that has had the bone removed before serving. Sometimes you can buy them ready-boned, but the silvery skin is always left on during cooking. If you prefer, both the salmon and the peppers can be cooked on a barbecue rather than under the grill.

darnes of grilled salmon with peppers and tomato and basil dressing

Serves 6

3 large yellow peppers, quartered

3 large red peppers, quartered

3 tbsp olive oil

6 x 150g salmon cutlets

sea salt and freshly ground black pepper

For the dressing:

3 ripe plum tomatoes, skinned,
  de-seeded and chopped

2 large cloves garlic, crushed

1 shallot, finely chopped

150ml olive oil

2 tbsp red wine vinegar

3 tbsp half-fat crème fraîche

8–10 large fresh basil leaves, shredded

Recommended wine: Palette from
  Provence

1 To make the dressing, put the chopped tomatoes, garlic and shallot in a food processor and blend to a purée. With the machine running, slowly add the olive oil and then the vinegar. Season. Mix in the crème fraîche. Pour the dressing into a bowl and stir in the shredded basil. Set aside.

2 Preheat the grill to very hot. Cook the pepper quarters, skin side up, for about 5 minutes until blackened and blistered. Remove, cover with a clean cloth and leave to cool. Peel off the skins, then cut the flesh into 1cm squares and put in a bowl. Mix with half the olive oil, then season and set aside.

3 Brush the remaining oil over the salmon cutlets and season them. Grill for about 3–4 minutes on each side until the flesh feels just firm, but not too hard. Now, using a sharp pointed knife, stab the central bone of each cutlet and firmly pull it up and out of the fish. The bone should pop out. (Alternatively, pull the bone out with your fingers.) Push the cutlet flesh back together to reshape.

4 Place the salmon on plates and spoon over the peppers. Shake the dressing once more, then trickle it over the fish. Serve warm.

This supper dish makes a good choice for a casual party meal, as most of the elements can be prepared ahead of time. You can cook the lentils and bacon, blanch the spinach and mix the dressing in advance, leaving only the fish to be baked. New potatoes or garlicky mash would go very well with this.

baked cod with lentils, leeks and mustard dressing

1   Put the lentils in a bowl and cover with cold water. Leave to soak for 1 hour, then drain and rinse. Transfer to a saucepan and add the bay leaf, onion slices, carrot and stock. Bring to the boil and cook over a medium heat for 10 minutes, then cover and gently simmer for 15 minutes or until tender. (Add very small amounts of boiling water if you need extra liquid.) At the end of cooking, there should be no liquid left, but drain off any that remains. Remove the bay leaf, onion and carrot. Season and set aside.

2   In another saucepan, heat two-thirds of the butter with 2–3 tablespoons of water and cook the diced leek for about 5 minutes until softened. Season, then mix into the lentils. Heat a non-stick pan and dry-fry the bacon until crisp and browned, then mix into the lentils. Season, especially with pepper.

3   Blanch the spinach in a pan of boiling water for 1 minute until just wilted. Drain immediately, rinse in cold water and drain again. Squeeze any excess water from the leaves, then season. Roughly chop and dot with the remaining butter.

4   Shake together all the ingredients for the dressing with some seasoning in a screw-top jar. Set aside.

5   Just before cooking the fish, preheat the oven to 190°C/375°F/Gas Mark 5. Then heat a large, shallow ovenproof pan on the stove and add the oil. Toss the cod fillets in the seasoned flour and shake off the excess. When the oil is hot, slide the fish fillets into the pan. Cook for 2 minutes, without moving the fish or it will break up. Then carefully turn with a palette knife or fish slice and place the pan in the oven. Bake for 5–7 minutes until the flesh feels just firm.

6   Meanwhile, reheat the lentils, leek and bacon in a saucepan. Reheat the spinach in a hot pan, or microwave, until the butter melts. Spoon the spinach on to a warm serving platter and arrange the fish fillets on top. Spoon over the lentils. Shake the dressing and drizzle over the whole dish. Serve hot.

Serves 6

200g Puy lentils

1 bay leaf

a few slices onion

1 small carrot

500ml Chicken Stock, Vegetable Nage
    (page 61) or Fish Stock (pages 58–59)

40g butter

1 large leek, finely diced

125g unsmoked back bacon, diced

400g spinach leaves, well washed

2 tbsp olive oil

6 x 150g cod fillets, skinned

2–3 tbsp seasoned flour

sea salt and freshly ground black pepper

For the dressing:

50ml white wine vinegar

150ml olive oil

2 tsp whole-grained mustard

Alternative fish: haddock, hake,
    swordfish

Recommended wine: Australian
    Chardonnay

I like to keep blends of whole spices in peppermills ready to grind on to a variety of fish and meats. One of my favourites is based on mustard seeds and is pungent and spicy. Another is more aromatic. Tuna tastes particularly good with the mustard-seed mix, especially when it is pressed into both sides of the richly flavoured tuna steaks before grilling.

spice-crusted tuna with chicory salad

Serves 6

6 x 80–100g tuna steaks, cut from
the loin

Chinese or Aromatic Pepper Mix
(page 40)

3 medium heads green and/or red
chicory, cored and thinly sliced

2 tbsp groundnut oil

For the dressing:

100g butter

2 tbsp groundnut oil

3 tbsp olive oil

3 tbsp sherry vinegar

2 tbsp clear honey

juice 1 small lemon

sea salt and freshly ground black pepper

Recommended wine: Fleurie

1   Trim the tuna neatly if necessary. Coarsely grind about 4–6 tablespoons of your chosen spice mix on to a flat plate. Press each side of the steaks into the mix, grinding more as necessary. It is not vital to cover the whole surface of the tuna. Chill the tuna in the fridge until ready to cook. Keep the sliced chicory in the fridge with the fish.

2   To make the dressing, melt the butter in a small saucepan. Increase the heat and, as soon as the butter starts to brown, remove from the heat. Take care not to let the butter burn. Pour through a sieve lined with wet muslin into a jug. This gets rid of the debris, leaving clear, nutty brown butter. Add the groundnut oil, olive oil, vinegar, honey and lemon juice, and season. Whisk well or shake in a screw-top jar to blend.

3   To cook the tuna, preheat a ridged grill pan, a barbecue or a top-heat grill until very hot. Dab the crusted tuna with the oil. Cook for about 3 minutes on each side until lightly firm and slightly springy. Season with a little salt and allow to stand for a few minutes while you mix the salad.

4   Toss the sliced chicory in half the dressing. Divide among six plates. Cut each tuna steak into thick slices and place on the salad. Trickle over the rest of the dressing and serve warm but not hot.

Considered to be one of the world's most beautiful fish, mahi mahi is usually caught in the waters of the Caribbean, although it is also found in the Mediterranean. Sometimes known as the dolphin fish, mahi mahi is usually sold as steaks, with the light-coloured flesh shaped in distinctive concentric rings.

mahi mahi with lemon grass and fennel

Serves 8

8 x 150g mahi mahi steaks

4 tbsp olive oil

3 stalks lemon grass, cut into 2cm
  lengths

1 tbsp fennel or dill seeds

small bunch fresh fennel or dill leaves

sea salt and freshly ground black pepper

Alternative fish: mackerel, tuna

Recommended wine: Chilean
  Chardonnay

1   Preheat the oven to 200°C/400°F/Gas Mark 6. Trim the mahi mahi steaks into a neat shape, cutting away any bruised flesh. Place in a single layer in a shallow ovenproof baking dish. Heat the olive oil in a small pan and add the lemon grass and fennel or dill seeds. Cook gently for a minute or two until the aromas rise from the pan.

2   Pour the infused oil and spices over the fish. Season well. Cover the dish with foil, then bake for 10–12 minutes, until the flesh is just firm when you press it.

3   When cooked, remove the foil and spoon the pan juices over the fish. Season again lightly, then set aside for 10 minutes to allow the flavours to develop.

4   Meanwhile, chop the fresh herbs. Scatter over the cooked fish and serve.

This dish can be served either as a starter or as a light main meal. You could also make smaller tarts for a picnic or buffet. Either way, it is a delightful mixture of smoked haddock, lentils and leek set in creamy egg. The tart is best served warm, with a simple green salad or vegetables.

smoked haddock, lentil and leek tart

1   To make the pastry, sift the flour, salt and paprika or mustard into a food processor. Add the butter and shortening, and process until the mixture resembles fine crumbs. Mix in trickles of ice-cold water, just enough to form a soft but not sticky dough.

2   Turn the dough out on to a lightly floured board. Knead lightly to a ball. Roll out to a circle large enough to line a 21cm loose-bottomed flan tin, 3.5cm deep. Line the tin, taking the dough well into the sides and pinching together any gaps, but do not trim the excess pastry as it will shrink back when cooked. Prick the bottom of the case with a fork, and line with non-stick baking parchment and baking beans for baking blind (page 218). Chill for at least 30 minutes while you make the filling.

3   Pour the milk into a saucepan and bring to a gentle simmer. Add the haddock and poach for about 10 minutes, or until the flesh just starts to flake. Remove the fish from the milk and flake the flesh, discarding skin and bones. Strain the milk and set aside.

4   In another pan, heat the butter and cook the leek for about 5 minutes until softened. (You may need to add a splash or two of water to prevent sticking.) Mix in the cooked lentils, flaked fish and chopped tomatoes. Season with pepper, but only a little salt because of the saltiness of the smoked fish. Allow to cool. Beat the whole eggs and egg yolks together, then mix in the cream. Stir in 150ml of the fish poaching milk and season well.

5   Preheat the oven to 200°C/400°F/Gas Mark 6. Place the flan tin on a baking sheet and bake the pastry case blind for 12 minutes. Carefully remove the paper and baking beans. Return to the oven to bake for a further 5 minutes. Remove, and reduce the oven temperature to 180°C/350°F/Gas Mark 4.

6   Using a sharp knife, trim the soft edges of pastry flush with the top of the tin. Spoon the haddock filling into the pastry case and spread evenly. Slowly pour in the egg and cream mixture. Return the tart to the oven and bake for 35–40 minutes, or until the filling is risen and golden brown. Allow to cool for about 15 minutes before removing from the tin. Cut into wedges and serve.

Serves 4–6

300ml whole-fat milk

500g undyed smoked haddock

25g butter

1 large leek, thinly sliced

150g cooked Puy or castelluccio lentils

2 plum tomatoes, skinned, de-seeded and finely chopped

2 eggs

2 egg yolks

300ml single cream

sea salt and freshly ground black pepper

For the pastry:

200g plain flour

½ tsp fine sea salt

1 tsp paprika or mustard powder

75g butter, chilled and diced

25g vegetable shortening

Alternative fish: smoked cod

Recommended wine: Montagny

I envy keen fishermen who can grill their own freshly caught mackerel. The flesh of the freshest mackerel is firm and full, and the stunning blue-grey skin so tantalizing. Its rich oiliness is well matched to these mustardy potatoes. You can grill the fish on or off the bone but, if cooking on the bone, you may like to score the skin on each side first and spike with spriggy herbs before cooking.

crispy grilled mackerel with warm mustard and chive potatoes

Serves 4

4 x 250g whole mackerel, gutted
   or filleted

good handful of herb leaves, such
   as rosemary, lemon thyme or
   summer savory

100ml olive oil + 1 tbsp for the fish

600g new potatoes, scrubbed

2 shallots, finely chopped

4 tbsp white wine vinegar

1 tbsp made English mustard

2–3 tbsp chopped fresh chives

sea salt and freshly ground black pepper

Alternative fish: fresh farm trout

Recommended wine: white
   Châteauneuf-du-Pape

1   Check that whole fish are well gutted, the gills removed, and clean inside and out. Make sure the dark blood line is well rinsed out. Cut off the heads, if you wish. Score the skin on both sides of each fish a few times and insert the herbs. Season lightly and brush with 1 tablespoon of the oil, then set aside. If using filleted fish, there's no need to score the skin, simply brush with oil.

2   Cook the potatoes in a saucepan of lightly salted boiling water until just tender. Drain. When cool enough to handle, cut into thick slices and set aside in the colander.

3   Pour the remaining oil into the same saucepan and add the shallots, vinegar, mustard and chives. Gently heat until warm, whisking to blend. Add the potato slices and stir gently to coat with the mixture. Remove from the heat and leave the potatoes in a warm place to infuse.

4   Preheat the grill to hot. If using whole fish, cook for about 5 minutes on each side. If using fillets, cook them skin side up, for about 5 minutes. Then, carefully turn over and grill the other side for 1–2 minutes, until just cooked. Check the seasoning, then serve the mackerel with the warm potatoes.

Snapper is something of a generic name when it comes to buying fish, although all fish which are sold under this name swim in warm waters, such as the Gulf of Mexico and the subtropical Atlantic. Whatever the type, be sure to choose a large fish with a pretty pink skin and full flavour for this recipe. Ask the fishmonger to scale and gut the fish and to leave the head on. The braised fish is best served warm, rather than hot, with crusty bread on the side.

braised snapper niçoise

1   Trim the snapper of fins and gills with kitchen scissors. Rub the fish all over with the oil and season lightly inside and out. Wrap the pancetta, if using, around the middle to hold the shape. Chill until ready to cook.

2   For the sauce, heat the oil in a saucepan and sweat the tomatoes and garlic, covered, for about 5 minutes until softened. Add the saffron strands and cook for a further 2 minutes until the mixture is quite pulpy. Pour in the wine and cook, uncovered, until reduced by half. Stir in the stock or nage and bring back to the boil. Season with salt and pepper, and add a good pinch each of sage and thyme and two or three tarragon leaves. Simmer for 5 minutes. Set aside until ready to cook the fish.

3   Preheat the oven to 190°C/375°F/Gas Mark 5. Place the snapper in a shallow roasting tin and spoon over the sauce. Bake for 5 minutes. Baste with a little of the sauce and return to the oven. Continue baking, basting every 5 minutes, for a total of 25–30 minutes, or until cooked and glossy. Check the flesh is cooked and flaky by opening it a little with a knife at the thickest part along the backbone.

4   Remove the fish and allow to cool slightly. Transfer to a large serving platter and scatter over the olives, if using. Garnish with the remaining sage, thyme and tarragon and serve with the sauce.

5   To carve a whole fish, use a long, sharp knife. Cut along one side of the backbone first, and gently work the blade down the ribs between the flesh and bones so the flesh comes away in a large fillet. Cut this fillet in two lengthways and place on plates. You should then be able to remove the fish's skeleton in one piece, lifting it from the tail like a kipper, to leave the second fillet underneath which you can cut easily from the head. If this cannot be done, turn the fish over carefully, and cut along the backbone and ribs to free the fillet as before. Discard the head (although some people like to eat the fish cheeks).

Serves 4

1 whole snapper, about 1kg, scaled
   and gutted
2 tbsp olive oil
4 slices cooking pancetta (optional)
10 pitted black olives, sliced (optional)

For the sauce:
2 tbsp olive oil
6 large plum tomatoes, skinned,
   de-seeded and chopped
2 large cloves garlic, crushed
good pinch saffron strands
150ml dry white wine
300ml Fish Stock (pages 58–59) or
   Vegetable Nage (page 61)
tips of fresh sprigs baby sage and thyme
   and a few leaves of tarragon
sea salt and freshly ground black pepper

Alternative fish: tilapia
Recommended wine: a light New
   Zealand Cabernet Franc

Lentils and seafood seem to have a natural affinity of colour, texture and flavour. This is especially true of dark Puy lentils, which look dramatic served alongside golden, crisp rings of squid. Cook the squid rings just before you serve, and enjoy this wonderful combination.

batter-fried squid with a spicy lentil salad

Serves 6

12 medium squid, prepared

300ml olive oil

1 tbsp balsamic vinegar

1 shallot, finely diced

1 fresh red chilli, de-seeded and
  finely diced

150g Puy lentils

25g butter

1 small carrot, finely diced

1 small leek, finely diced

2 rashers bacon, finely chopped

2 tsp white wine vinegar

sprigs fresh parsley, basil or snipped
  chives, to garnish

sea salt and freshly ground black pepper

For the batter:

15g fresh yeast, or 1 sachet easy-blend
  dried yeast

600ml milk, warmed to tepid

400g plain flour

1 tsp salt

Recommended wine: a Burgundy
  Pinot Noir

1   Cut the squid tubes into 2cm rings and pat dry with kitchen paper towels. Mix the rings and tentacles with 100ml of the olive oil, the balsamic vinegar, shallot and half the chilli. Set aside to marinate for about 2 hours.

2   Meanwhile, soak the lentils for 1 hour in cold water. Drain and cook in a pan of boiling water for about 15 minutes, or until tender. Drain and set aside.

3   In a frying pan, heat the butter and sauté the carrot, leek and bacon for about 5 minutes until softened. Mix into the lentils. Add 2 tablespoons of the remaining oil, the wine vinegar and the remaining chilli and season to taste. Set aside in a cool place to allow the flavours to develop.

4   To make the batter, blend the fresh yeast, if using, with 2 tablespoons of the tepid milk to a cream. Mix into the flour with the salt and the rest of the milk, using a balloon whisk or a food processor. If using dried yeast, mix it into the flour with the salt, then blend with the milk. Set aside for about 1 hour.

5   When ready to cook, drain the squid in a sieve. Heat the remaining oil in a frying pan until almost smoking. Dip a few of the squid rings and tentacles into the batter and drop straight away into the hot oil. Cook for about 2 minutes until golden brown and crisp, stirring carefully. Drain on kitchen paper towels. Repeat with the remaining squid and batter, reheating the oil between batches.

6   Spoon the lentil salad on to a serving plate. Pile the crispy squid on top and season. Garnish with sprigs of herbs – deep-fried or fresh – and serve.

This is a variation of the Smoked Haddock, Lentil and Leek Tart on page 187. Here soft, tangy goat's cheese and salty anchovies work surprisingly well together as a filling, especially when mixed with spinach and red onion. Serve the tart warm.

anchovy, spinach and goat's cheese tart

1   Make the pastry, then roll out and use to line a 21cm loose-bottomed flan tin, 3.5cm deep (follow the instructions in steps 1 and 2 on page 187). Chill for at least 30 minutes while you make the filling.

2   For the filling, heat the butter in a saucepan and sauté the red onion for about 5 minutes until just softened. Blanch the spinach in a pan of boiling water for 1 minute, then drain and rinse under cold running water. Drain well, squeezing out excess liquid. Mix the chopped spinach with the onion. Snip up the anchovies. Beat the goat's cheese with the cream, eggs, yolks and seasoning.

3   Preheat the oven to 200°C/400°F/Gas Mark 6. Bake the pastry case blind, following the instructions on page 218. When the pastry case is ready for the filling, turn the oven down to 180°C/350°F/Gas Mark 4. Spoon in the onion and spinach mixture, spreading it out evenly with a fork. Scatter over the snipped anchovies. Slowly pour in the cheese and egg mixture, then sprinkle over some freshly grated nutmeg. Bake for 35–40 minutes until the filling is risen and golden brown. Allow to cool for about 15 minutes, then cut the tart into wedges and serve.

Serves 4–6

25g butter
1 medium red onion, sliced
300g baby spinach leaves,
   roughly chopped
50g can anchovy fillets, drained
   and patted dry
300g soft goat's cheese
300ml single cream
2 eggs
2 egg yolks
freshly grated nutmeg to sprinkle
sea salt and freshly ground black pepper

For the pastry:

200g plain flour
½ tsp fine sea salt
1 tsp paprika or mustard powder
75g butter, chilled and diced
25g vegetable shortening

Recommended wine: a light Italian
   Barbera

Fresh sturgeon would be a good talking point at a party – and it is cheaper than caviar, at least. It is now available as farmed fish but, being meaty, it tends to be a little on the dry side. A good way to get around this is to marinate it overnight in olive oil, and avoid overcooking. Sturgeon comes into its own served with this classic beurre noisette sauce and tender new potatoes.

sturgeon with brown butter, lime and caper sauce

Serves 6

6 x 150g sturgeon fillets, skinned

2 tbsp olive oil

2 large fresh limes

100g butter

2 tbsp capers, drained and patted dry

1 tbsp chopped fresh parsley

1kg new potatoes (e.g. Jersey Royals)

100g clarified butter (page 218)

sea salt and freshly ground black pepper

Recommended wines: white
  Hermitage, Gérard Chave

1   Marinate the sturgeon in the oil overnight. You can do this in a polythene food bag.

2   Using a canelle knife, take the zest from the limes in fine strips and set aside. Alternatively, cut the peel thinly using a swivel vegetable peeler, and cut into fine strips. Squeeze the lime juice into a bowl and set aside.

3   Put the unclarified butter in a shallow saucepan and heat until it starts to brown. As soon as it reaches this point, stop the cooking by adding the lime juice and then the strips of zest and the capers. Season, stir in the parsley and set aside.

4   Cook the potatoes in their skins in a pan of lightly salted boiling water. Drain and, when cool enough to handle, peel off the skins and slice the flesh. (You can wear clean rubber gloves to protect your hands when doing this.)

5   Heat the clarified butter in a frying pan. Just as it starts to turn brown, add the potatoes. Fry for about 10 minutes until golden brown. Transfer to a serving plate.

6   Heat a large frying pan and, when very hot, slide in the sturgeon fillets. Cook on one side for 3 minutes until browned. Carefully turn over and cook the other side until the flesh feels lightly springy. Season. Reheat the sauce, then serve the fish on the bed of potatoes with the sauce spooned over.

accompaniments

This simple way with rice is foolproof and also very tasty. It is important to choose a good brand of Indian basmati, as the quality of the rice can vary greatly. If using a high-quality basmati it is not essential to rinse it before cooking, although this does make the rice grains lighter.

spiced rice pilaff

Serves 4

250g basmati rice

1 tbsp olive oil or sunflower oil

1 small onion, chopped

1 clove garlic, crushed (optional)

1 large green chilli, de-seeded and
   chopped (optional)

1 tbsp grated fresh root ginger (optional)

1 tsp Aromatic Pepper Mix (page 40)

knob of butter (optional)

500ml Vegetable Nage (page 61),
   Chicken Stock (page 61) or water

1 tsp sea salt

1–2 tbsp chopped fresh parsley
   or coriander

1   Put the rice in a large sieve and rinse under cold running water for a good minute or two, turning the grains with your fingers. Leave the rice to drain in the sieve.

2   Meanwhile, heat the oil in a large pan. Add the onion, garlic, the chilli and ginger, if using, and the aromatic pepper mix, and gently fry for about 5 minutes until the onion has softened. Add the butter, if using. When it has melted, stir in the rice and cook for about 1 minute, still stirring.

3   Pour in the nage, stock or water. Bring to the boil and stir in the salt. Stir the rice once or twice, then reduce the heat to low and cover the pan. Cook at a gentle simmer for 12 minutes without lifting the lid.

4   At the end of the cooking time, remove the pan from the heat and leave to stand for 5 minutes. Uncover the pan and gently fluff up the grains with a fork. Mix in the chopped herbs. Spoon into a serving dish and serve.

Variation

Saffron pilaff: put a good pinch of saffron strands in a cup or small bowl and pour over 1–2 tablespoons of boiling water. Leave to soak for about 10 minutes. Trickle the saffron over the cooked pilaff before fluffing up the grains. The rice should be speckled with yellow and white.

Smooth mashed potatoes are indispensable to fish dishes. To make a mash that is memorable requires some attention to detail. First, choose a potato variety such as the King Edward, Maris Piper or Estima. La Ratte, a French variety, is also good if you can get hold of it, because it is slightly sweet and starchy, yet quite firm when cooked. Its pale yellow flesh makes wonderful mash. Boil the potatoes in their skins and peel straight after cooking. This produces the ultimate flavour. Never be tempted to cut corners by puréeing the potatoes in a food processor – you are likely to end up with a gluey mess.

potato purée

1   Cover the potatoes with cold water in a saucepan. Bring to the boil, then simmer for 15–20 minutes, or until the flesh is tender when pierced. Drain in a colander. Wearing rubber gloves, peel the potatoes while still hot.

2   To purée, either push the cooked potatoes through a fine metal drum sieve, or round sieve, using a plastic spatula, or use an old-fashioned potato ricer (the type that looks like a large square garlic press).

3   Meanwhile, heat the milk in a saucepan. Beat the butter into the mashed potato (adding any of the flavourings suggested below) and season to taste.

4   Just as the milk comes up to the boil, remove from the heat and beat into the potatoes. Add dribbles of extra milk if necessary. (Bear in mind the texture of the accompanying dish before adding more. Dishes with a lot of sauce need a firmer texture, while pan-fried or grilled fish will benefit from a softer purée.) Keep the purée warm until ready to serve.

Serves 6
1kg good-quality potatoes,
   (e.g. La Ratte, King Edward, Estima or
   Maris Piper), well scrubbed
about 100ml milk
up to 4 tbsp butter
sea salt and freshly ground black pepper

Flavourings

Basil mash: either beat in some Fresh Basil Purée (page 75) which colours the purée, or steep fresh basil leaves in the hot milk for 15–20 minutes, then discard the leaves and beat into the potatoes. Alternatively, simply trickle in a little basil-flavoured oil.

Garlic mash: mix in some Roasted Garlic Purée (page 215) to taste.

Mustard mash: mix in 2–3 teaspoons of coarse-grained mustard. This mash goes well with full-flavoured fish.

This is a classic French side dish, but I make it slightly differently. Traditionally, fondant potatoes are cut as thick cylinders and caramelized gently in butter and stock. I use thinner slices, about 2cm. You will need a heavy-based, non-stick frying pan that is wide enough to take the potatoes in a single layer. Use a light stock or water, with extra to hand in case you need to top up the level. The trick is to make sure the potatoes reach the right degree of tenderness just as they turn a deep caramel colour.

fondant potatoes

Serves 6

about 800g medium potatoes, peeled
50g butter
3 fresh thyme sprigs
2 small bay leaves
300–450ml Vegetable Nage (page 61),
　Chicken Stock (page 61) or water
sea salt and freshly ground black pepper

1　Trim the potatoes into neat cylinder shapes, then cut into 2cm slices. Discard the ends, or use to make mash (page 199).

2　In a large heavy-based frying pan, warm the butter very gently until just melted, then remove from the heat. Arrange the potato slices in a single layer in the melted butter, fitting them together like a jigsaw puzzle. Season, sprinkle over the thyme sprigs and add the bay leaves.

3　Pour in enough nage, stock or water to come just halfway up the potatoes. Return the pan to the stove and cook over a medium to low heat until the liquid bubbles gently. Cook, uncovered, on a gentle bubble for about 15–20 minutes, or until the butter turns a light brown and the liquid has almost completely evaporated. The potatoes should be a deep golden brown on their undersides.

4　Carefully flip the potato slices over, using a palette knife. Pour in more nage, stock or water, again halfway up. Cook for a further 15–20 minutes until the liquid has evaporated and the potatoes are tender, deep golden brown and caramelized. Drain on kitchen paper towels, season and serve as soon as possible.

Cabbage is a good all-round accompaniment, rarely served with fish, but I urge you to try it. Use a crinkly two-tone green Savoy cabbage for this recipe. Instead of boiling it in the conventional way, use this method of lightly sweating it in a little butter. The addition of fresh marjoram and aromatic cumin seeds makes the most of the cabbage's flavour and texture.

braised cabbage with marjoram

1   Quarter the cabbage and slice off the core. Pull off any tough outer leaves, then finely shred the rest of the cabbage.

2   In a large saucepan, heat the butter and gently cook the shallot or onion for about 5 minutes until softened. Take care not to let it colour.

3   Pile in the cabbage and stir well. Cover and cook over a gentle heat for about 4–5 minutes, shaking the pan once or twice, until wilted. If you find it needs a little water, then add just a splash or two during cooking.

4   Stir in the cumin and marjoram, and season to taste. Replace the lid, then remove from the heat and leave to infuse for a few minutes. Mix in cream to taste and serve.

Serves 4–6

1 small to medium Savoy cabbage

25g butter

1 shallot or small onion, finely chopped

good pinch cumin seeds or ½ tsp
   ground cumin

1 tbsp chopped fresh marjoram

1–2 tbsp double cream

salt and freshly ground black pepper

These are an elegant accompaniment for fish dishes. They can be prepared an hour or two ahead, then lightly warmed before serving. They are made in the same way as classic apple tarte tatin, using buttery puff or shortcrust pastry. I make them in individual metal moulds, about 8cm in diameter, heated on top of the stove to caramelize the chicory heads. They can then be baked in the oven with their pastry cases in place. Instead of the moulds, you can use deep muffin tins, sold in trays with 9 or 12 cups. Loose-bottomed flan tins are not suitable as the juices from the chicory will seep out.

tatins of chicory

Makes 12

300g homemade pastry (page 187)
   or good-quality ready-made puff
   pastry or shortcrust pastry

80g caster sugar

100g butter, softened

½ tsp five-spice powder

6 small, fat heads of chicory, about 100g
   each, cored and trimmed

sea salt and freshly ground black pepper

1   Roll out the pastry on a lightly floured board and cut out twelve discs, each about 8–9cm in diameter. Prick well with a fork and set aside in the fridge.

2   Meanwhile, in a bowl, cream together the sugar, butter, spice powder and a little seasoning. Preheat the oven to 200°C/400°F/Gas Mark 6, and put a metal baking sheet in the oven to warm. (This will help to brown the tatin bases.)

3   Cut each head of chicory in half lengthways. If the half heads start to fall apart, gather the leaves together and secure each with a wooden cocktail stick.

4   Spoon half the creamed butter and sugar mixture into a heavy-based frying pan. Spread it around a little, then press the chicory halves, cut side down, into the pan. Heat gently at first, then, as soon as the juices start to seep out, raise the heat. Add any stray leaves to the pan. Cook for about 7 minutes until the mixture starts to caramelize and the chicory starts to soften and wilt. Try not to move the chicory heads too much; they are best left in place.

5   Meanwhile, divide the remaining butter and sugar mixture among the moulds or muffin tins. As soon as the chicory halves begin to soften, remove them with a spoon or fork, one at a time, to each mould, placing them cut side up. Pack the stray chicory leaves in around the heads.

6   Lay a pastry round on top of each chicory half, pressing well down and round the chicory rather than pressing on to the metal of the tin. Place the tin on the preheated baking sheet. Bake for 12–15 minutes or until the pastry rounds are crisp and golden and the chicory is softened. Cool for a few minutes, then turn out on to a serving dish, pastry side down. Carefully transfer the juices from the moulds or tins to a jug, pour over the warm tarts and serve.

Fish with spinach is like a marriage made in kitchen heaven. This sublime mixture of cheese and spinach is incredibly simple to prepare, and can be served with any grilled or pan-fried fish.

gratin of spinach and gruyère

1   Pick off any thick stalks from the spinach. Bring a pan of water to the boil, and plunge in the leaves for only a few seconds until the spinach wilts. Drain, then refresh under cold running water. Drain well again and set aside. When cool enough to handle, squeeze the leaves dry by hand. Chop into small pieces.

2   Heat the butter in a saucepan and add the spinach, cream, nutmeg and seasoning. Heat, stirring, until the mixture starts to hiss – just a minute or two. Spoon into a serving dish and sprinkle over the Gruyère cheese.

3   Preheat the grill to hot, then cook the spinach until the cheese is golden brown and bubbling. Cool for a few minutes, then serve.

Serves 4

200g young spinach leaves, washed
   thoroughly and drained
20g butter
1–2 tbsp double cream
a little freshly grated nutmeg
50g Gruyère cheese, grated
sea salt and freshly ground black pepper

Lentils make good partners for any fish or shellfish, but particularly salmon, sea bass, langoustines and scallops. Serve the lentil and bacon mixture either hot or at room temperature, but never chilled, as if it is too cold the flavour will be diminished.

lentils and bacon

Serves 4

150g Puy lentils, washed thoroughly
  and drained

2 medium carrots

1 medium leek

1 shallot, cut in half

1 bay leaf

1 bouquet garni (page 39) (optional)

1 tbsp olive oil

50g smoked bacon, cut into
  small lardons

2 tbsp Classic Vinaigrette (page 76)

sea salt and freshly ground black pepper

1   Soak the lentils for 1 hour in cold water. Drain. Place the lentils in a saucepan with one of the carrots, the green part of the leek, half the shallot, the bay leaf and bouquet garni, if using. Cover with cold water and bring to the boil. Cover and simmer gently for 15–20 minutes, or until the lentils are just softened but still whole. Drain and discard the vegetables, bay leaf and bouquet garni. Set the lentils aside.

2   Meanwhile, finely chop the remaining carrot, white of leek and shallot half. Heat the oil in a saucepan. When hot, add the bacon and cook for a minute or two until the fat is released. Add the chopped vegetables and stir to mix. Cook over a medium heat for about 5 minutes, or until softened. Season lightly, then remove and mix with the lentils and vinaigrette. Serve hot or warm.

Cauliflower may seem an unlikely accompaniment for fish dishes, but this creamy purée really does provide a perfect complement. One way of using it, as I have done in the recipe on page 123, is to drop small spoonfuls of the purée on to plates and nestle pan-fried scallops or small fish fillets on top. It is not essential to include the truffle oil, but it certainly adds a richness to the finished flavour.

cauliflower purée

Serves 6–8

1 small cauliflower

25g butter

2 tbsp milk

100ml single cream

a little truffle oil (optional)

sea salt and freshly ground black pepper

1   Trim the cauliflower into small florets, leaving only a small amount of stalk on each.

2   Melt the butter in a saucepan. Add the florets and cook gently for about 3 minutes until lightly softened. Add the milk and cook for another 2–3 minutes. Season lightly. Pour in the cream and return to a gentle boil. Partially cover the saucepan and cook for another 3 minutes, or until the florets are softened, but not pulpy.

3   Tip the cauliflower and all the juices into a food processor and blend to a smooth purée, scraping the sides of the container down once or twice. Trickle in the truffle oil to taste, if using. For a wonderfully smooth and glossy texture, let the food processor run for a while. Check the seasoning and serve.

These meltingly delicious tomatoes can be served with salads or as a garnish for grilled whole fish. Allow one whole tomato per person and serve cool or at room temperature. They also make a delicious accompaniment to poached Finnan haddock served with a nice mound of buttery mashed potato.

slow-roasted tomatoes

1   Cut the tomatoes in half lengthways and remove the cores. Lay cut side up in a shallow roasting tin.

2   Preheat the oven to 150°C/300°F/Gas Mark 2. Brush the tomatoes with the oil first, then trickle over the vinegar. Season well.

3   Roast, uncovered, for about 2 hours, or until softened but still whole. Leave to cool in the tin. Remove carefully to a serving dish and drizzle over a little more olive oil, if needed. Sprinkle with the herbs, if using, and serve.

Serves 8

8 ripe, firm plum tomatoes or large
    vine-ripened tomatoes
2 tbsp extra-virgin olive oil
2 tbsp balsamic vinegar
fine sea salt and freshly ground
    black pepper
chopped fresh herbs of your choice or
    thyme leaves to garnish (optional)

I use these tangy tomato crisps to garnish many dishes and, like all good ideas, this recipe is deceptively simple. Wafer-thin slices of tomato are dried on a non-stick silicone sheet overnight, then stored in an airtight box. (Various brands of these sheets, such as Dupont Teflon, Bake-o-Glide and Magic Carpet, are available in most major supermarkets or through mail-order.) You will need a razor-sharp knife to slice the tomatoes wafer thin. The crisps will keep for a week or so in an airtight tin.

oven-dried tomato crisps

1   Using a razor-sharp knife, cut the tomatoes crossways as thinly as possible. Discard the ends. Lay out the slices on a plastic silicone sheet or baking parchment on a baking sheet. Season well with sea salt and pepper.

2   Turn the oven to its lowest setting, such as the plate-warming or slow-cook setting. Use a wooden spoon to prop open the oven door if necessary so that it is slightly ajar. Place the tomato slices in the oven.

3   Leave the tomato slices to dry, which can take anything from 4 to 24 hours. (The timing depends on your oven.) Do not turn the slices. When the tomatoes are completely dry and crisp, they are ready. Peel them off the sheet and store in an airtight container, ready for use.

Makes 30–40 slices

6 ripe, firm plum tomatoes
fine sea salt and freshly ground
  black pepper

This is a kind of mushroom hash used by French chefs for stuffing, garnishing or stirring into sauces. It is wonderful as a flavouring for fish. There are a few tips to prevent duxelles from turning into a dark mess. First, take the time to chop the mushrooms by hand. If you use a food processor you will bruise the mushrooms and the duxelles will turn black. The next tip is to use a dry heavy-based frying pan, making sure it is really hot before cooking. This will ensure that the mixture itself is nice and dry.

duxelles of mushrooms

Makes about 400g

500g selection of clean, dry
   mushrooms (e.g. chanterelles,
   champignons de Paris, button
   mushrooms, ceps or morels)
fine sea salt

1   Pick over the mushrooms carefully and wipe clean with kitchen paper towels, if necessary, making sure they are completely dry.

2   Chop finely with a very sharp knife, taking care not to bruise the flesh.

3   Heat a large heavy-based non-stick pan. When you can feel a good steady heat rising, tip in the chopped mushrooms. Sprinkle over some salt. Gradually the mushrooms will give up their liquid. Stir the mixture frequently as the liquid seeps out. Cook for 5–8 minutes until all the liquid has evaporated and the mixture is rich and thick. Cool and use as required.

A small jar of ready-to-use garlic stored in the fridge is useful whenever you need to boost the flavour of sauces, stuffings or marinades. After all, you might as well peel several heads of garlic at a time and roast them to be used straight from the jar. Spoon the cooked purée into a small screw-top jar and pour a thin layer of olive oil on top to prolong the storage life. The purée should keep well for up to 10 days, but you may need to add some more olive oil occasionally if it starts to look a little dry. Choose heads of garlic with plump cloves and discard any that have started to yellow or, even worse, turned to a grey powder.

roasted garlic purée

1   Separate the cloves of garlic and peel each clove. To peel garlic easily, place the cloves, one at a time, on a board and position a large heavy-bladed knife flat on top. Clench your fist and smash down hard on to the flat blade. This will loosen the skin of the garlic clove which can then be removed easily. Snip off the stalk ends and roughly chop any very large cloves.

2   In a small pan, heat the butter and oil with the garlic cloves. Gently sauté for about 1–2 minutes, or until the garlic cloves turn a light golden colour.

3   Pour in the stock, nage or water and bring to the boil. Place a butter wrapper or sheet of crumpled wet greaseproof paper on top. Turn the heat down and simmer for 10–15 minutes, or until the garlic cloves are softened, shaking the pan once or twice.

4   In a food processor, whizz the garlic and pan juices to a smooth purée. Spoon into a clean screw-top jar and cover the surface with a thin layer of olive oil. Cool and then seal, using as required.

Makes about 100ml

4 large heads of garlic

25g butter

1 tbsp olive oil

100ml Fish Stock (pages 58–59),
  Vegetable Nage (page 61) or water

I like to make a batch of these lemon slices and then press one or two on to fish fillets when pan-roasting or grilling for a brilliant blending of flavours. Store in a screw-top jar in the fridge for up to a fortnight.

candied lemon

Makes about 20 slices

2 large unwaxed lemons, well scrubbed

100g caster sugar

1 stalk fresh lemon grass, split in two

1   Top and tail the lemons. Using a razor-sharp knife, cut each one crossways into about 10 thin slices. Set aside.

2   Dissolve the sugar in 300ml water in a saucepan over a gentle heat, stirring occasionally. When no crystals remain, add the lemon grass. Increase the heat and gently boil for 1–2 minutes. Add the lemon slices, stirring well, then remove from the heat. Set aside to cool.

3   Pour the lemons and their syrup into a screw-top jar. Use as required.

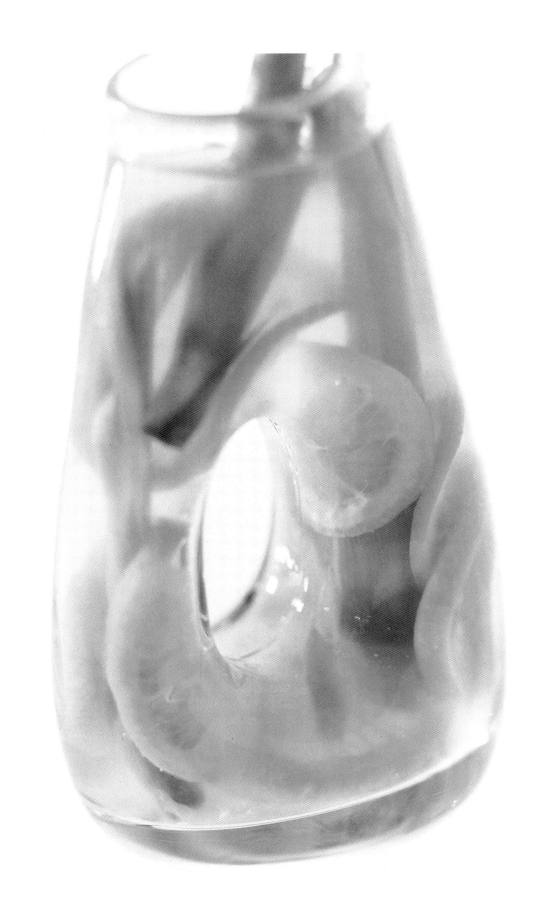

glossary

bain-marie A receptacle used for gently cooking food or a delicate sauce that might curdle or split if cooked too fiercely. The food is placed in a container that sits in or above a water bath with a temperature of 100°C/ 212°F (which is the bain-marie). This can take place in the oven or on the stove. We cook light mousses in oven bain-maries and certain sauces on the stove in double saucepans.

bake blind This involves baking a pastry case without a filling so that it becomes light and crisp. After rolling out the pastry and lining the tin, rest the pastry case in the fridge for 30 minutes or so. Then line the pastry case and fill with ceramic or baking beans. Do not trim the edges of the pastry case until halfway through baking; that way they will not shrink back too much. Preheat the oven to 200°C/400°F/Gas Mark 6. Place the tin on a heavy metal baking sheet, to transmit more heat, and bake for 15 minutes. Remove the lining and beans, then return the pastry case to the oven and bake for a further 10 minutes to crisp up. Continue with the recipe chosen or cool the flan case and fill with cream, fruits etc.

blanch To dip food into boiling water or very hot fat to cook briefly. Blanching in boiling water is often followed by refreshing. We blanch and refresh green vegetables and raviolis, and reheat them briefly in a little buttery water before serving. Homemade chips are best fat-blanched at approximately 150–160°C/ 300–325°F, until cooked but still pale. Then they are removed whilst the temperature of the fat is increased to 180–190°C/ 350–375°F to brown and crisp them.

brioche crumbs Preheat the oven to 150°C/300°F/Gas Mark 2. Cut a stale brioche loaf into fine slices, and spread them out on the oven shelves. Bake for about 1 hour until the bread is pale golden and quite crisp. Remove and cool, then break into pieces. Whizz in a food processor to make very fine crumbs. Sieve the crumbs to remove any large lumps. Tip these back into the processor and whizz again, if liked. If you can't find brioche, use good-quality white bread or Italian breadsticks (grissini), but avoid using packets of artificially coloured crumbs.

chillies The seeds in chillies are even more fiery than the flesh, so some recipes advise you to remove them. To do this, slit the chilli lengthways, then simply scrape out the seeds. You may wish to wear thin rubber gloves, as chilli juice can sting if you rub your eyes or mouth afterwards.

clarified butter Use a 250g pack of butter because, once clarified, it will keep for several months in the refrigerator. Gently melt the butter in a saucepan, or in a bowl in a microwave on a medium setting. Line a sieve with a piece of muslin or a clean J-cloth and set over a bowl. Slowly pour in the melted butter, leaving as much of the milky solids behind as possible. What you are left with is almost pure butter fat. When using to fry, add 1–2 tablespoons of olive oil or sunflower oil, as melted butter, even when clarified, burns easily.

concassé (tomatoes) Skin the tomatoes (see easy-peel method), cut into quarters and de-seed, then cut the flesh into strips and finely dice.

de-glaze After we fry meat or sauté shallots, we add a little wine or wine vinegar to the pan to loosen the meaty deposits. The liquid bubbles away almost instantly, but its flavour is left behind.

easy-peel method To skin tomatoes or peel baby onions or shallots quickly, dip them in a pan of boiling water for a minute, then drain and rinse under cold water. The skins will slip off easily. With tomatoes, cut out the core. You can then quarter them to scoop out the seeds, if necessary.

julienne This term is applied to food (generally vegetables) cut into long, very fine strips. It is named after a well-known eighteenth-century Parisian chef, Jean Julien, who added fine vegetable strips to consommé. To make them, you need to have a very sharp cook's knife. Cut the vegetable first into long, thin rectangles, about 2.5mm thick. Stack 3 or 4 rectangles on top of each other, then slice into shreds about 1mm thick. With practice you'll soon be able to do them quite quickly. Julienne strips of vegetables are often blanched for just a minute and then refreshed. This softens them and they can be used as a wispy garnish.

lardons These are small cubes of bacon, lean or fatty, smoked or unsmoked. Use them to add flavour to stews and casseroles, or fry until crisp and then toss into a salad of mixed leaves (Salade Mesclun).

lemon grass It is important to make sure the lemon grass you buy is fresh and juicy and not dried out. To prepare it, peel off the outer layer and trim the top. Slit the stem from the root end to the tip so that it is like a brush. Then scissor snip the halved stem into fine pieces. You will release lots of fresh aroma this way. Once the sauce or dressing has been made, the lemon grass can be strained out. This stage is important as lemon grass can be quite tough if it is only lightly cooked.

nappé (coat) A term used to describe covering a small item of food evenly in a velvety-smooth sauce. The angle the spoon is held at is important. Fill the spoon with sauce, then tip it from the side (not from the tip), working front to back so the sauce flows gently and evenly over the food to be coated.

pavé This term, taken from the French word for paving stone, is used to describe a slice of terrine, mousse or parfait.

peeling peppers In some restaurants peppers are grilled or roasted before peeling. This gives them a smoky flavour and softens the flesh. If you want to avoid this, peel peppers with a swivel vegetable peeler. Do this whilst they are still whole, then cut them in half.

quenelles Use two teaspoons to make these neat shapes. Scoop up the mixture on one spoon. Twist and turn the other spoon into the bowl of the first spoon, transferring the mixture from the first spoon to the second. This action smooths the top of the mixture. Repeat this several more times until you have produced a neat torpedo shape. Gently shake the quenelle on to a serving plate.

refresh To dip blanched vegetables or pasta into ice-cold water to stop any further cooking and to set the bright colour.

sabayon A light, frothy egg sauce. A sabayon is generally sweet (like a fluffy Zabaglione dessert), although we also make savoury sabayons by beating egg yolks with seasoning before whisking in cubes of butter as for a light Hollandaise sauce. This makes the sauce more stable. Sabayons are whisked over a stove-top bain-marie using either a large balloon whisk or an electric beater.

scallop coral powder We remove corals from scallops before cooking. But little is wasted in my kitchen, so we use the corals to make a powder for adding wonderful colour and flavour to sauces and risottos. Slice the corals in half horizontally and clean if necessary. Line a baking sheet with non-stick silicone film (the plastic type that is reusable, not paper parchment). Place the corals on this in a single layer. Set them in the oven on the lowest setting possible, such as the plate-warming setting. In the restaurant kitchen our ovens have gas pilot lights which are ideal for long, slow drying. You may need to prop open your oven door even on its lowest setting. Leave the corals to dry for anything between 8–16 hours until the corals are dark orange and very brittle. They should snap in two. Now the noisy bit. Place a few at a time in a food processor and whizz until you have a fine powder. The noise is deafening, but it's worth it. Store the powder in a screw-top jar in a cool, dark place.

weights and measures

solid weight conversions

metric	imperial	metric	imperial
15g	½ oz	225g	8oz
25g/30g	1oz	250g	9oz
40g	1½ oz	275g	9½ oz
50g	1¾ oz	300g	10½ oz
60g	2¼ oz	325g	11½ oz
75g	2¾ oz	350g	12oz
85g	3oz	375g	13oz
100g	3½ oz	400g	14oz
115g	4oz	425g	15oz
125g	4½ oz	450g	1lb
150g	5½ oz	500g	1lb 2oz
175g	6oz	1kg	2lb 4oz
200g	7oz		

liquid conversions

metric	imperial	metric	imperial
15ml	½ fl oz	400ml	14fl oz
30ml	1fl oz	425ml	15fl oz/¾ pint
50ml	2fl oz	450ml	16fl oz
75ml	2½ fl oz	500ml	18fl oz
100ml	3½ fl oz	568ml	1 pint
125ml	4fl oz	600ml	20fl oz/ 1 pint
150ml	5fl oz/¼ pint	700ml	1¼ pint
175ml	6fl oz	850ml	1½ pint
200ml	7fl oz/⅓ pint	1 litre	1¾ pint
225ml	8fl oz		
250ml	9fl oz		
300ml	10fl oz/½ pint		
350ml	12fl oz		

alternative fish

Alternative names for the same species of fish are given here, as well as some suggested substitutes in brackets (if any). French names are also given as these are often used on restaurant menus.

fish

british	french	american	australian
Anchovy	Anchois	Anchovy	Anchovy
Brill	Barbue	Brill, (Petrale Sole)	Flounder, Sole
Cod	Cabillaud, Morue Fraiche	Cod	New Zealand/Blue Cod
Conger Eel	Congre	Conger Eel	Grenadier
Dover Sole	Sole	Dover Sole	Sole, Flounder
Gilt-head Bream	Daurade	(Sea Bream, Porgy)	Sea Bream
Haddock	Eglefin	Haddock	Blue Cod, Hoki
Hake	Merlu	Hake	Gemfish
Halibut	Flétan	Halibut	Grouper, Gemfish
Herring	Hareng	Herring	Sardine
John Dory	St Pierre	John Dory	John Dory
Lemon Sole	Sole Limande	English Sole, (Flounder)	Flounder
Ling	Lingue	(Cusk)	Ling
Mackerel	Maquereau	Mackerel	Mackerel
Mahi Mahi	Coryphene Commune	Mahi Mahi, Dolphin Fish	Kingfish
Marlin	Makaire	Marlin, Sailfish	Marlin
Monkfish	Lotte	Monkfish, Anglerfish	Monkfish
Plaice	Carrelet, Plie	(Flounder, Sole)	Flounder, Sole
Red Mullet	Rouget	(Goatfish)	Barbounia
Salmon	Saumon	Salmon	Atlantic and Pacific Salmon
Sardine	Sardine	Sardine	Sardine
Sea Bass	Bar, Loup de Mer	Sea Bass	Grouper
Skate	Raie, Pocheteau Gris	Skate	Skate
Snapper	Bourgeois	Snapper	Sea Bream
Sturgeon	Esturgeon	Sturgeon	Sturgeon
Swordfish	Espadon	Swordfish	Swordfish
Tuna	Thon	Tuna	Tuna
Turbot	Turbot	Flounder	Flounder
Whiting	Merlan	Whiting, (Silver Hake)	Whiting

shellfish and other seafood

british	french	american	australian
Clam	Palourde, Praire	Clam (various)	Clam (various)
Cockle	Coque	Cockle	Pipi, Cockle
Crab	Tourteau	Crab	Crab
Dublin Bay Prawns	Langoustine	Norway Lobster, Jumbo Shrimp	Scampi, Yabbie
Lobster	Homard	Lobster	Lobster
Mussel	Moule	Mussel	Mussel
Oyster	Huître	Oyster	Oyster
Prawn	Crevette	Shrimp	Prawn
Scallop	Coquille St. Jacques	Sea Scallop	Scallop
Sea Urchins	Oursin	Sea Urchin	Sea Urchin
Squid	Calmar, Encornet	Squid	Squid, Calimari
Winkle	Bigorneau	Periwinkle	Winkle

... and caviar is the same in almost all languages!

index

author's acknowledgments

I would like to thank Roz Denny for her great patience.

Thank you to Kate Bell and Leslie Harrington for their endless effort, and a very special thank you to one of the most talented food photographers in the country, Diana Miller. Thanks also to Carla, my assistant, for trying to get me to meetings on time.

A chef is only as good as the brigade that works alongside him. My special thanks go to Mark Askew, one of the most consistent and talented young chefs who ever stepped into my kitchen as chef de cuisine. He has the strong support of Richard Wood and Nathan Thomas, the youngest chef of my brigade; Darren Vaughan's demonstration of techniques in wrapping the brill in layers of potato deserves loud praise.

My five years' working relationship with my suppliers has gone from strength to strength. Ours is a great example of a complete understanding between supplier and kitchen. The consistent quality of the produce is evident in all the photographs, particularly with the caviar of Ramin Rohgar of Imperial Caviar, the wonderful fish of Laky Zervudachi of Rockport, Tunbridge Wells, and Steven Bird of Cove Shellfish, Bournemouth.

I could not miss out Greta, my mother-in-law, for providing me with a handful of wonderful recipes, like her special chowder, and giving me the excuse to prove how a domestic homestyle dish can be turned into a professional recipe.

Finally, to Tana and Megan: thank you for being there.

publisher's acknowledgments

The publisher would like to acknowledge the following for their invaluable assistance: photographer's assistants Leo Acker and Vanessa Later; James Hayward for his help with the step-by-step photography; Lizzie Harris and David Peacock; Penelope Cream and Jane Royston for editorial assistance; and Hilary Bird for the index.